KNOWLEDGE, ATTITUDE, & EXPERIENCE

MINISTRY IN THE CROSS-CULTURAL CONTEXT

YOUNG-IL KIM

EDITOR

ABINGDON PRESS
NASHVILLE

KNOWLEDGE, ATTITUDE, AND EXPERIENCE:
MINISTRY IN THE CROSS-CULTURAL CONTEXT

This book is printed on acid-free recycled paper.

Library of Congress Cataloging-in-Publication Data

Knowledge, attitude, and experience : ministry in the
  cross-cultural context / edited by Young-IL Kim.
        p.   cm.
    ISBN 0-687-27041-3 (alk. paper)
    1. Pastoral theology. 2. Cultural relations. I. Kim, Young-IL,
1941–
BV4011.K62 1992
253—dc20
                                                                    92-8589
                                                                        CIP

Manufactured in the United States of America

This project was originally undertaken to commemorate the fifth anniversary of the Center for Asian-American Ministries at Garrett-Evangelical Theological Seminary, but it has taken much longer than planned.

We hope that this collection of articles will help people open their eyes and minds to the deeper and wider dimensions of cultures different from their own. We have prepared this resource to be used in various settings: for seminary courses dealing with cross-cultural issues in ministry, for parish ministers, educators, and laypersons who seek a tool to equip the local church for more effective ministry, and for the general reader, who will find in these pages a stimulus to nurture changing attitudes. The motive behind this book is to awaken people to the cross-cultural context all around us.

I am deeply grateful to all of the contributors for their interest and courtesies extended during the preparation of the manuscript. Without their willingness to work on this project in the midst of their many other responsibilities, this volume could never have come to fruition. Finally, special thanks are due Barbara Smith Jang for her invaluable assistance. She gave much time, attention, and insight to improving the organization of the book, and her very significant contribution is acknowledged with affection and respect.

C ONTENTS

Identifying and Communicating God's Presence in the Cross-Cultural Context

—Young-IL Kim

After three years of study in the United States at Phillips Theological Seminary, I was appointed to serve as the pastor of Ransom and Bethel United Methodist churches, a two-point charge in rural Pennsylvania. Ransom, an isolated country village surrounded on three sides by mountains and on the south by the Susquetianna River, is about fifteen miles southwest of Scranton and ten miles south of Clarks Summit. All of the cultural, educational, and employment opportunities available to the people of Ransom and Bethel were located in those larger towns. Ransom did have a convalescence home, a small post office, and a paper mill. The village consisted of about twenty homes along Main Street and another fifty homes scattered around on the crossroads and in the valleys. The ethnic makeup of the community was German, Scottish, Polish, Irish, Italian, and Swiss—all European. Ransom was a remote town, insulated from the ethnic diversity and cultural opportunities of urban America.

When I was appointed to serve the Ransom and Bethel charge, ours was the first Asian family *ever* to live in that community. We felt like a freak show or an exhibit at the zoo. The people were extremely curious about us. They came to look, to talk with us, to ask us questions. I could see the inquisitiveness in their faces and sensed their desire to understand us in their endless rounds of questioning. During my first year there, many people came to church out of curiosity, to hear me speak, or to hear what I had to say.

7

Since the founding of the Ransom church 150 years before, I was their first noncaucasian pastor. My presence there stimulated their curiosity about Asian culture. They began to open their eyes and their minds to learn about other cultures. For example, while I was serving there, the Ransom church held a program in which we invited about thirty migrant workers, mostly African Americans, to come to the church for a dinner put on by the United Methodist Women, followed by a time of dialogue. This was a very special event for the church members. For many, it was their first direct encounter with blacks. The people of Ransom had, of course, heard of Asians and Africans, but actual face-to-face contact with people of other cultures had been limited or nonexistent. As their awareness and understanding of other cultures increased, they gained a better sense of their own culture and began to appreciate their own traditions. They began to see themselves through the lens of the other cultures. This cross-cultural experience was very meaningful for them and for their self-understanding. It shed new light on their 150-year history and self-image.

This idea of understanding oneself more clearly by understanding others was introduced by Charles Horton Cooley (1864–1929) in his book *Human Nature and the Social Order* (New York: Charles Scribners, 1902, 1922, 1956). Cooley held that we see ourselves as others see us. We continually see ourselves in a mirror created by the actions and reactions of members of society who react to us and interact with us. Cooley's theory of the "looking-glass self" suggests that the image we have of ourselves is that image which is reflected to us in a mirror. Nearly everyone looks in a mirror every day. I regularly see my reflected image and internalize a picture of my appearance based on what I see in the mirror. By looking at my reflection, I recognize that my hair is graying, that my skin is blemished, and I visualize myself accordingly.

In the same way, other people are looking-glasses that

surround us in society. Many people don't recognize others as mirrors; but nevertheless, they react to the reflections given them by those others. Family, friends, and colleagues tell one another what they like or dislike about their personalities or appearances. They comment directly or indirectly about one another's intelligence, attractiveness, and competence. People react to that feedback and formulate their self-images on that basis. A clear example of this is how children act out the roles that they perceive their parents describing for them based on their parents' reactions to them and their comments to others about their children's behaviors and personalities.

This is the "social looking-glass." I believe that the individual is linked to society chiefly through the looking-glass self. Who we are to ourselves, Cooley argued, is a social product, the result of feedback from how others see us. So the looking-glass is a dramatic metaphor for the way society's image of us gets incorporated into our own self-image. Through social feedback and comparison of ourselves with others, we gain self-understanding, self-appreciation, and self-knowledge. Just as one can use a mirror to apply cosmetics to alter one's physical appearance, so can a person use the social mirror to try to change his or her social image by altering behaviors, adopting new ways of thinking and acting, or eliminating undesirable attributes as perceived in the reflection. Or, just as someone can smash a mirror out of self-hatred or frustration with the appearance reflected, a person can reject the image imposed upon him or her by society by refusing to live according to commonly accepted social rules or assumptions.

The use of a single mirror provides a reverse-image, a two-dimensional, frontal perspective. In a barber shop, the barber uses two mirrors to show how the hair is cut on the back of the head. Three mirrors are used in a clothing store to display the new clothing from many angles. The added dimensions create a more complete, more realistic picture of the subject. Likewise, a monocultural community tends to reflect a one-dimensional image of the members of the community, whereas a multicultural community reflects many more dimensions of the self in a greater variety of ways, leading to deeper self-understanding and a more complete picture of the self in relation to others. In the interaction of an ethnically diverse society, one culture can be altered or re-created through contact with other cultures. As individuals or communities reflect on such feedback from significant others, attributes of the self come into focus. Other people and cultures can act as mirrors providing us with a picture of who we are. Self-awareness is clearly obtained through looking at others, allowing us to broaden and improve our self-conceptions.

The people in the small village of Ransom really appreciated me. My presence provided them with an opportunity to re-create and adopt new self-images and new ways of living. They learned about, reflected on, and evaluated themselves. Some folks would look at our life-style and say, "Wow, that's wonderful. Let's try to be more like that." For example, many people came to appreciate the Korean practice of removing one's shoes upon entering a house, and some adopted that custom. Some reevaluated their eating habits and incorporated more Asian cuisine into their meal plans. Others were amazed at our children's modest and self-disciplined behavior. They'd tell one another, "Look at Kim's kids," and would want to know how we reared them and what the differences were between Korean and American culture. But the increasing self-understanding which led to the alteration of their self-image and appreciation of their own culture was perhaps the most important effect. Some said, "Gosh, I'm glad I'm not Asian," or "I'm glad I *am* such-and-such," or "I'm glad I know how to do thus-and-so." The point is that exposure to another culture led to more complete self-knowledge.

10

Theological Education

Cross-cultural awareness has been a new trend in theological education and ministry since the 1980s. More and more conferences and denominations require new pastors to be equipped with cross-cultural skills, such as knowledge of the issues and experience in cross-cultural ministry. American society, to which clergy and laity alike minister, is a picture of ethnic diversity. Until recently, United States society was composed primarily of European and African immigrants, but now Latin American and Asian immigrants are adding new components to the pluralism of this society.

The Center for Asian-American Ministries was established at Garrett-Evangelical Theological Seminary (G-ETS) in the fall of 1984. Before that, there had been only three to five Asian students on campus at any one time. G-ETS as an institution did not recognize the need to be concerned about the Asian American component of American society or of its student body. Now that the seminary does officially promote cross-cultural education and ministry, and actively recruits Asian and Asian American students, the number of Asian students has dramatically increased to sixty-six (in 1991–92). This represents an increase of Asian students from 0.8 percent of the total student enrollment across all degree programs in the 1983 academic year to more than 17 percent now.

I see people from various cultures freely interacting on the G-ETS campus. Faculty and students alike appreciate learning, reflecting, interacting, and sharing with the Asian student presence, as well as with other students from a multitude of cultural backgrounds. Their presence here has led to a heightened awareness of the need for cross-cultural skills in ministry. One of the special emphases at G-ETS now is on cross-cultural education.

This trend toward internationalization of theological education and preparation for cross-cultural ministry is happening in

11

many seminaries across Canada and the United States. The thirty-sixth biennial meeting of the Association of Theological Schools (ATS) organized a "Task Force on Globalization" in 1986 and declared the 1990s the "Decade of Globalization." The Committee on Internationalization of Theological Education had previously been established in 1980 to begin addressing the need for more global awareness and understanding to be incorporated into theological education.[1]

G-ETS is a good example of this trend in theological education. G-ETS organized its own Committee for Internationalization soon after the ATS committee was established. The "Church and the Black Experience Center," which had earlier been established at G-ETS, in 1970, "helps the seminary to integrate the black experience into the total life of the seminary community. It also attempts to model both conceptually and experientially the inclusive Church, and it seeks to equip African-American seminarians with skills that exemplify quality leadership in today's pluralistic Church."[2] The Center for Hispanic Ministries was established in 1988 "in response to the urgent need for more ordained and diaconal leaders for churches in the Hispanic community . . . and acts as a conduit, bringing Hispanic culture and experience into the life of the seminary."[3] Most recently, a requirement has been added to the M.Div. and M.C.E. curriculum that all students must have some cross-cultural experience, either overseas or in alternative United States cultures. The need for cross-cultural skills in ministry is there. G-ETS is attempting to equip students to meet the new challenges in ministry effectively and efficiently.

There is another reason why cross-cultural ministry is becoming increasingly important. Before air travel became commonplace, the world was a huge place. Asians had virtually no opportunity to travel to Europe or North America. When my father-in-law came to the United States to study in the 1930s, he spent weeks on a ship to get here.

Later he traveled by propeller airplanes, which had to stop and refuel often, so the trip took several days. Now the flight from Seoul to Chicago is a matter of hours. It's amazing how small the world is becoming. When I was a boy, going to Europe or the United States was considered a lifelong dream; now it is just a matter of making vacation plans.

Technology has made the globe much smaller. Crossing cultures is now commonplace. Accordingly, there is an increased possibility for the peoples of the world to become one small town, one community, one family. Isn't true understanding of one another, loving concern and care the ultimate goal of Christianity? Isn't it the ultimate will of God? Geographically the world is much smaller, but culturally we are still worlds apart. Structurally we have a colorful mix of culture and ethnicity in our society, but we lack a real crossing of cultures, a giving and receiving, learning from and understanding of one another. The door to cognitive interaction is still closed. People are unwilling to interact on any more than the superficial level.

Thus the need for cross-cultural skills in ministry is great. This anthology of essays is an attempt to help meet this need. I propose a triangular approach to the study of cross-cultural communication. The three corners of the triangle are knowledge, attitude, and experience. They meet in the circular center section as cross-cultural interaction. All three aspects are needed for healthy cross-cultural ministry. Knowledge alone without a change in attitude does not make for good ministry. The correct attitude without any experience or knowledge is insufficient preparation for cross-cultural ministry. Experience alone, without understanding or a healthy attitude, does not an effective minister make.

As the diagram on page 14 suggests, the central, circular area as approached by knowledge, attitude, and experience is the core of cross-cultural energy and power. When all three aspects of preparation for cross-cultural ministry are brought

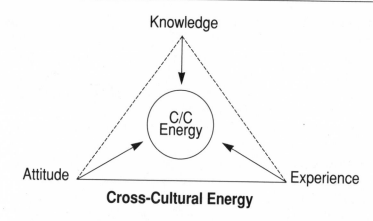

Cross-Cultural Energy

together in the center, there is a power. Any one aspect alone is not enough. The three together make for a wholeness, a totality, a powerful energy.

This book brings together nine essays, which address different aspects of these three dimensions of cross-cultural ministry. The first dimension, which deals with knowledge, or the importance of the need for cross-cultural awareness to be processed more actively, is addressed in the articles by Robert Jewett, Rosemary Radford Ruether, and W. Richard Stegner. The second group of essays, dealing with the dimension of attitude, includes articles by James B. Ashbrook, Young-IL Kim, Edward P. Wimberly, Nolbert Kunonga, and Douglas E. Wingeier ("The Ministry as Cross-Cultural Communication"). This dimension not only stresses the enlarging of our perspectives but also requires an altering of attitude, a mending of our minds. The third dimension, experience, is addressed to some extent in most of these articles, but is specifically addressed by Douglas E. Wingeier ("Learning About Ministry from the Two-thirds World"). Experience enriches our minds and broadens our horizons.

Let me now introduce the articles in this anthology. Articles that primarily address the dimension of knowledge in cross-cultural ministry include "Competing in the Creedal

Olympics: Pauline Resources for Cross-Cultural Ministry,"
by Robert Jewett. In this essay, Dr. Jewett examines the
creed found in Romans 1:1-5. In today's cross-cultural
community, the Christian community is divided into many
groups. Likewise, the creed found in Romans contains
contributions from three sources. Jewett first explores these
different contributions and then examines Paul's approach to
this plurality of the early Christian church. Jewett forms
these conclusions:

1) A strong Jewish-Christian influence is found. It is a
   conservative view, emphasizing nationalistic hopes and
   desires.
2) An equally strong contribution is made by the "liberal,
   charismatic theology of the Hellenistic churches."
3) Paul makes his own contributions, modifying and
   moderating the two extreme views represented by the
   Jewish-Christian and the Hellenistic branches of the
   church.

We see the competition of different elements in this creed.
Which wins out, the nationalistic or the ecumenical version?
Jewett maintains that there are no firsts save Christ. In this
plurality, there is a harmony in the unity of Christ. Jewett
presents us with some knowledge of the Bible's cross-cultural
past to aid us in finding some solutions for the problems of the
present.

Also in the vein of contributing to knowledge of
cross-cultural contexts, Rosemary Radford Ruether writes
concerning the development of feminist theology in the
Third World. I recently had an awakening experience that
helped me to recognize that cross-cultural differences are
also experienced in terms of gender. In August 1991, I
participated in the World Gathering of United Methodist
Clergy Women in Chicago. I sat there all day as the only male

15

with the Korean clergywomen's delegation, which included about twenty-five women from Korea and twenty-six Korean American women. As a seminary faculty member who deals regularly with the issue of sexism, I had thought of myself as being very understanding and empathetic of the issues faced by women clergy, much more so than the average male clergyperson. But that day I was awakened and felt myself merging with the pain, frustration, and struggles of the women clergy. I recognized that day that this too is a cross-cultural issue. The element of experience is crucial here. Even though I had often talked about the role of women clergy and their struggles and joys, until I physically immersed myself in their gathering I didn't feel their issues with my heart. Thus the actual experience of living in cross-cultural settings is a vital part of seminary education and preparation for effectiveness in any kind of ministry.

This book is about helping people understand one another. The article by Dr. Ruether addresses this issue. This essay describes the history and some of the significant characteristics of feminist Third World theology. Only recently has such theology begun developing. In the 1970s, feminist theology was almost entirely restricted to white Western women, while the liberation theologies were developed by organizations in the Third World such as the Ecumenical Association of Third World Theologians (EATWOT). It was in the 1980s that the cry for women's voices to be heard started to gain momentum. This was the emergence of the Third World feminist theologies within the liberation theologies. This liberation feminism shares several common aspects. It protests the patriarchalism of the church and examines the historical aspects of social, economic, and political oppression and how it relates to the present.

The article by W. Richard Stegner, "Recent Religious Developments: A New Testament Theological Perspective," is a theoretical piece that contributes to our understanding of

16

the rapid growth of the church in the Third World and particularly in Asia, and how that illustrates the continuing work of God in history. This insightful article contributes to our collective knowledge about the cross-cultural context for practicing ministry.

Attitude, the second dimension of cross-cultural energy, is addressed in the sermon "Strangers and Foreigners" by James B. Ashbrook. The Reverend Dr. Ashbrook speaks of the attitude of the emigrant (or immigrant) faith. Through his examination of the book of Hebrews, he addresses the uncertainty of the immigrant. What or who is an immigrant? Immigrants are strangers and foreigners. An immigrant is one who is uprooted to find himself or herself in a strange land. What are the characteristics of the immigrant condition: isolation, alienation, fear, loneliness, uncertainty? It can be and often is all of these, but the immigrant life is also one of faith. The immigrant life is the story of faith. Ashbrook states that "we are called to travel." The immigrants' call is God's call, and we are all immigrants, even if one's family has lived in the same place for many generations. We are called to be "people-on-the-move" in a world in which we do not belong. This is the path to Christ. This immigrant faith is the Christian faith.

Also falling primarily under the category of "attitude" is Young-IL Kim's article "God's Dream for a Technicolor Society." Dr. Kim constructs an immigrant theology by looking at what is perhaps the paradigm of intercultural interaction, United States society. The history of the United States is one of immigration, and this essay begins with the history of North American immigration as waves of successive immigrants. Kim then goes on to examine various theories of assimilation. Whether one adheres to the melting pot theory, the triple melting pot, or the idea of pluralism, all these theories attempt to take into account the existence and interaction of the many diverse ethnic groups that constitute the United States. The

17

history of immigration is then compared to the parable of the vineyard in the twentieth chapter of Matthew. Like the late workers in the vineyard, each successive wave of immigration has often been met with resentment and suspicion. Ultimately it is not a question of fairness but comes down to God's grace, which belongs to everybody.

Edward P. Wimberly also addresses the issue of attitude in his article, "A Narrative Approach to Pastoral Care in an Intercultural Setting." Teaching and learning in theological education often tends to be very analytic, conceptual, and abstract. This is the ocular approach academia utilizes so well and so often, but this is not the only way to learn about or view the world. In an intercultural setting, Dr. Wimberly asserts that it is important not to forget the oral approach, which is an integral part of so many non-Western cultures. Theology can be a strange new language to some students, a way of looking at the world in a manner entirely different from that to which they are accustomed. It does not fit snugly into their experiential realities. But this need not be true. The oral or narrative approach can be used to draw "personal ways of learning and experiencing reality into the academic process." This allows an integration of the student experience. In contrast to the ocular approach, this narrative approach is relational, subjective, and concrete. It is the use of metaphor, image, and story. It is the use of one's own story to relate to the story of Jesus.

Another approach to attitude is taken by Nolbert Kunonga, an Anglican priest from Zimbabwe who is currently studying for an advanced degree at G-ETS. The Reverend Mr. Kunonga integrates the uniquely African concepts of existence-in-relation, *Guruuswa,* or the center where all humans come into being, and the stomach as the locus of empathy and social solidarity, into a theology and a style of cross-cultural ministry.

The African God, *Mwari,* exists in relation with people and the whole community, endures the pain of humankind, and

18

forms the model for the minister as wounded healer. Christ both suffers with people and also acts to reverse and re-order social evil and injustice. The African pastor, a victim of the racism of a colonial culture, joins with Christ in this liberating activity. Cross-cultural ministry, based in the African concept of existence-in-relation, becomes both empathy with suffering and action to overcome its causes and transform the world.

Concluding the set of articles addressing the issue of attitude is Douglas E. Wingeier's piece entitled "The Ministry as Cross-Cultural Communication." Dr. Wingeier draws from his vast cross-cultural experience to offer a practical guide to the proper attitudes for cross-cultural ministry. He asserts that *"all* ministry is essentially cross-cultural communication," and that our central challenge is to interpret the ancient words of the Bible into meanings relevant to the various cultures that compose today's society. Paul's doctrine of *kenosis* is essential in this regard. *Kenosis* entails an emptying—in this context an emptying of cultural assumptions and the willingness to take on those of another. What is important is that we learn to shed our cultural arrogance and be willing to don the robes of cultural humility, the attitude that we can always learn from others. We must be willing to *ask, listen,* and *witness,* important basic skills and tactics for cross-cultural ministry.

The third dimension of cross-cultural awareness, that is, experience, serves as the basis for the final article, "Learning About Ministry from the Two-thirds World," also by Dr. Wingeier. We often become complacent and isolate ourselves from the rest of the world. We suffer delusions thinking ourselves superior to "the others" materially, mentally, and spiritually. After all, didn't we have to teach them everything? Wingeier thoroughly rejects this view as he draws from his own invaluable experiences in the other "two-thirds" of our world. More specifically, he speaks of what he has learned from his travels in Western Samoa,

Korea, China, and Nicaragua. Each society exists and grows in its own unique environment and consequently will have different things to offer. What can we learn from other cultures? That is the question Wingeier asks as he himself seeks to contribute to their learning. In the hierarchically structured culture in Western Samoa, one sees the importance of service as a path to authority. The practices of the Korean church show the necessity of regular prayer and accountability, while the Korean Shamanistic tradition teaches us the joy we can find in mystery and the inspiration to "protest against injustice and oppression." One learns of the courage and faithfulness of the Chinese church as they battled through persecution, and one finds lessons of solidarity and struggle in the Base Christian Communities of Nicaragua. We all learn from our experiences, but we can also learn from the experiences of others.

This book is written for clergy, laity, and educators. All three aspects of cross-cultural communication—experience, knowledge, and attitude—need to be addressed in our various ministries. We need a sense of urgency to obtain this element of cross-cultural energy. This energy is needed by pastors, laity, and educators to maintain a balance, because knowing and having only monoculture means imbalance. The Bible teaches that we are sisters and brothers in God and we need to share effectively. To do so, we need the energy that comes from holistic cross-cultural foundations.

Notes

1. Committee on Internationalization of Theological Education, *ATS Bulletin,* 1982, no. 35, pp. 98-110.
2. G-ETS 1989–92 catalog, p. 73.
3. Ibid.

PART ONE:
KNOWLEDGE

Competing in the Creedal Olympics: Pauline Resources for Cross-Cultural Ministry
—Robert Jewett

In this article, Robert Jewett exegetes and discusses one example of a biblical resource for cross-cultural ministry. Jewett describes the Olympic and Pauline forms of the ecumenical ideal, both of which provide resources to understand the task of cross-cultural ministry today. In Paul's case, the creed cited in Romans 1:3-5 is shown to be a composite in which an originally conservative, Jewish-Christian creed had been edited by liberal Gentile-Christians. Paul holds the creed together after making two small corrections, framing it with explicit references to the lordship of the transcendent Christ. The creed thus honors cultural diversity, yet provides a transcendent framework within which to hold such diversity together. A similar embodiment of an ecumenical ideal was seen in the 1988 Olympics in Seoul where the Cha Chun Game used in the opening ceremonies was transformed in a remarkable manner to bring it close to the Pauline vision. This article provides a fascinating example of biblical exegesis that reveals the cross-cultural currents of early Christianity and applies them to our modern situation.

Dr. Jewett is the Harry R. Kendall Professor of New Testament Interpretation at Garrett-Evangelical Theological Seminary. His interest in discovering biblical resources for cross-cultural ministry surfaced in his first book, Paul's Anthropological Terms: A Study of Their Use in Conflict Settings *(1971). Subsequent studies have dealt with distortions in cross-cultural relations, particularly his study* The Captain America Complex: The Dilemma of Zealous Nationalism *(1973,*

23

1984) and a series of articles in the Christian Century *running from 1973 to the present. His book that builds the most explicit positive rationale for cross-cultural ministry is* Christian Tolerance: Paul's Message to the Modern Church *(1982). A technical monograph published in 1986,* The Thessalonian Correspondence: Pauline Rhetoric and Millenarian Piety, *offers a fascinating glimpse of cross-cultural misunderstanding within the early church. Jewett's current research is devoted to a commentary on Paul's letter to the Romans, from which the ideas in the current article were drawn. He was educated in a cross-cultural context, receiving degrees from Nebraska Wesleyan University, the University of Chicago, and the University of Tubingen in Germany. Dr. Jewett has taught at Garrett-Evangelical since 1980.*

The gospel . . . concerning his son,
   "born of David's seed
     according to the flesh,
   appointed son of God in power
     according to the spirit of holiness,
   through the resurrection from the dead,"
Jesus Christ our Lord, through whom we have received grace and apostleship for the obedience of faith among all the nations.   (Rom. 1:3-5 author's trans.)[1]

T he last several times our family watched the Olympic Games on television, I found myself thinking about the project of placing Pauline texts in the context of what the philosopher Josiah Royce called "the beloved community."[2] That such a community contains cross-cultural elements is implicit both for the Olympics and for the church. There is a sense in which both the Olympics and the Pauline vision of the church share an ecumenical ideal and offer rich resources for the understanding of ministry in cross-cultural settings. The letter to the Romans was written while Paul was at Corinth, the site of one of the most important Greek parallels to the modern Olympics, the Isthmian Games. We know from the athletic imagery in Paul's letters that he had incorporated some of the Olympic ideals into his own thought, expanding and transforming them in unique ways.

In the ancient as in the modern games, one ran or threw the javelin for his own city or country; the immense popularity and wealth of successful athletes was directly related to chauvinism, the desire to have one's city triumph over others. The competing cities of the ancient world were comparable to the teams marching under national flags in our modern Olympic Games. Consequently, there was a continuing tension between the Olympic ideals of a partially unified human race, consisting of course only of freeborn males who could speak Greek, and the glory of one's particular city. A similar tension was manifest at Los Angeles in 1984, when the playing of the national anthems alternated with occasional moments when the entire colosseum blossomed with the flags of other nations, magically created from colored sheets under the seats of spectators at the opening ceremony, or when people actually followed the admonition to "reach out and touch someone" from somewhere else. There were symbols of an ecumenical vision in the 1988 Olympic Games at Seoul, South Korea, that were even more impressive.

We experience a related tension within the larger Christian community in the United States. Coming from as many different traditions as we do, and marching under rather diverse theological banners, it seems at times as if we worship different Christs. Some of us are charismatics, some traditionalists, some conservatives, and some liberals. Yet we celebrate one Lord and one faith, symbolized in the one loaf in which we are all united. Is this unity merely in our minds? Does it have the power to transcend our flags?

These are the questions Paul was wrestling with in his letter to the Romans, addressed to a church splintered by racial and theological conflicts.[3] That is why the creed he cites in verses 3-4 of chapter 1 in Romans is so intriguing. As reconstructed by recent research, this early Christian creed consists of at least three levels of creative, editorial activity, each reflecting the flag of a different group in the church.[4] Paul's method of coping with different kinds of creeds may provide some suggestions about how we might approach pluralism not only in our churches but also in America and the world community.

The earliest level of the creed Paul cites in Romans bears the marks of the conservative, Jewish-Christian branch of early Christianity. In a parallel formulation whose balance is more visible in the original language than in modern translations, they confessed belief in Jesus:

> born of David's seed,
> appointed son of God through the resurrection from the dead.
> (author's trans.)

There are three distinct colors in this creedal flag, so to speak. Up front was the nationalistic hope, a kind of bright scarlet. For Jewish-Christians still loyal to the ancient homeland, the messiah had to represent the restoration of the Davidic dynasty in one form or another. Just as for modern nations whose loyalty to their flags stands in some relation to their struggles for independence and self-identity, so the confession "born of David's seed" conveyed hope for a downtrodden people. In one way or another, it involved release from the exploitation and domination of the empire. It conveyed a strong sense of racial identity and even of racial superiority, for David's restored dynasty was to rule over the Gentiles.

Closely related to this nationalistic emphasis was the

26

reference to Christ's being "appointed son of God." The technical term for a royal decree used in the Old Testament appears here: For example, listen to the wording of Psalm 2, which uses this technical language: "I will tell of the *decree* of the Lord:/He said to me, 'You are my son;/today I have begotten you./Ask of me, and I will make the nations your heritage,/and the ends of the earth your possession./You shall break them with a rod of iron,/and dash them in pieces like a potter's vessel' "(Ps. 2:7-9, emphasis added).

If such a destiny was to be fulfilled, it would have to come from divine intervention. Jesus' adoption as the son of God was seen as the indisputable sign of divine authority in the new age, transcending every limitation of current power arrangements, the true blue color of the Jewish-Christian flag.

The third color in the original creed was the white flash of the Resurrection: "appointed son of God through the resurrection from the dead." As in the other early creeds, the emphasis on the resurrection of Christ was central. As Paul confesses in I Corinthians 15, if Christ had in fact not been raised, "our proclamation has been in vain and your faith has been in vain . . . your faith is futile and you are still in your sins . . . [and] we [Christians] are of all people most to be pitied" (vv. 14-19). I think the same could be said for today, whether for modern liberals or for conservatives: The Christian faith makes no sense without the foundation of Jesus' resurrection.

So there we have it—the scarlet, white, and blue creed of the conservative Jewish-Christians. Like it or not, it is part of the heritage of United Methodism as well as part of the shared faith of a broad stream of the ecumenical movement. It is strongly nationalistic, supportive of conservative moral values, insistent on the literal belief in the bodily resurrection of Jesus. It is also noncharismatic. And it is represented to some degree in the evangelical heritage of this seminary. One component of this early creed is closely associated as well with the recovery of a strong sense of racial and national identity both here and abroad. The Church and the Black Experience Center here at Garrett-Evangelical would fly this scarlet, blue, and white flag just as proudly as the United Church of India or the indigenous churches of Asia or Africa.

What makes the confession in Romans intriguing, however, is that more than one creedal flag was flying. Recent research has made it likely that another branch of the early church added some key lines to the original creed. The words "according to the flesh" and "according to the spirit" substantially alter the original intent of the creed, shifting it in the direction of the liberal, charismatic theology of the Hellenistic churches. The contours of what I am going to describe as a purple-and-pink flag assume a sharply polemical focus.

When the phrase "according to the flesh" was added to the line "born of David's seed," a negative qualification was made. Both in Hellenistic Judaism and in the branch of Christianity influenced by Paul, the realms of flesh and spirit were thought to be radically opposed. Flesh was viewed as the sphere of darkness and damnation; spirit was the sphere of redemption and light. To live "according to the flesh" was to allow yourself to be reduced to limited human resources, while life "according to the spirit" was thought to be open to divine power. Such power was felt to be manifest in the charismatic worship of some branches of the early church. To say that Jesus was "born of David's seed *according to the flesh*" reduced the business of royal ancestry to something intrinsically opposed to the spirit. It was like negative points in the Olympic diving or gymnastic contests.

The liberal branch of early Christianity that drew the purple field called "according to the flesh" in the flag apparently wished to discredit the nationalistic hopes in the

28

Jewish-Christian creed. They felt that the new faith was international in its implications. They opposed the jingoistic impulses such as Jewish or Davidic superiority. This branch of the early church favored an ecumenical ideal. In a sense, they resonated with the original vision of the Olympic Games, where nationalistic conflicts would be set aside while individual humans submitting to divine rules sought to reach universally recognized heights of prowess and speed.

The pink color in the liberal banner was writ large with the letters "according to the spirit." They added this line to make the antithesis between flesh and spirit complete, thereby indicating where the real power of salvation erupted and how it was conveyed. To confess that Jesus was "appointed son of God *according to the spirit*" embodied the claim that the spirit-filled experience of believers far surpassed the physical origins of Jesus. The channel of the divine voice, speaking to him in the baptism experience with the words "You are my beloved son," was open to every Christian, according to the Hellenistic Christians. Their own experience of the spirit represented access to the new age, so the true significance of Jesus was in making the spirit available to all. Their experience is related to modern experiences of charismatic revival that some groups within the church today treasure.

"Not according to the flesh, but according to the spirit"—that kind of slogan has long been part of our liberal, Wesleyan heritage. It has kept some branches of our church open to charismatic religious experience and has provided a critical principle by which the church and society could be reformed. Current cross-cultural ministry must learn to honor the purple and pink banners as well as the ones with red, white, and blue. Yet the question will always reemerge, Which banner should prevail? Whose side deserves the golden moment on the dais with their creedal anthem playing and an adoring world looking on to see if there are tears on solemn cheeks?

29

Paul's answer is surprising, given his well-known sympathies with the purple-and-pink banner of liberal, spirit-filled Christianity and his frequent conflicts with flag-waving Jewish nationalists. He allows both banners to fly side by side in the creed cited in verses 3-4, adding only a couple of unobtrusive qualifications that scholars have detected. It is as if he wanted to place a modest orange-and-green flag next to the banners that others had mounted.

The first of these was the insertion of a little phrase in the line concerning Jesus' appointment as "son of God." Paul added the words "in power" to the confession of the enthronement: "appointed son of God in power . . . " I feel that this is something of a correction to the claims of the Jewish-Christian creed, which laid so much emphasis on Davidic origins. The ultimate power for Paul derives not from nationalistic and dynastic continuity but rather from the divine decree that appointed Jesus to his unique status.

Power is a crucial theme in Romans, with the thesis in 1:16-17 stressing that the gospel "is the power of God for salvation." The Good News about Christ's life, death, resurrection, and enthronement is the most powerful force on earth, according to Paul. Nations and flags may rise or fall; guns and bombs may destroy; swift legs may set new world records; but only the gospel has the power to redeem the lost. Only the message about the love of God manifest in Christ can set the guilty free. And apart from proclaiming the transcendent power of God there is no hope for keeping human arrogance and folly within bounds, to save the foolish world or wanton individuals from self-destruction. This is why Paul stresses the visibility of divine "power" in Romans 1:20, arguing that when persons fail to recognize it, they fall into a self-imposed darkness. This is why Paul includes other "powers" in the list of factors unable to "separate us from the love of God in Christ Jesus our Lord" in Romans 8:38-39. This is why he returns to the theme of divine power in the

30

benediction of Romans 15:13. "May the God of hope fill you with all joy and peace in believing, so that you may abound in hope *by the power* of the Holy Spirit" (emphasis added).

If we did not believe that the gospel of Christ embodies the greatest power on earth, none of us would be involved in ministry. If the students at our seminary had not been touched by this power, they would not have left professions and homes and former relationships to devote themselves to the study of Christian ministry, whose center is the power of the gospel. We celebrate that power in the Lord's Supper, in which Christ meets us as Lord. He establishes his power-sphere as we eat and drink at this table, conveying to us once again that the most powerful force on earth is his self-giving love. "This is my body which is for you . . . this is my blood, shed for you and for many." Committed to that body, Paul inserted the words "in power" to make plain that no national flag and no Davidic descent can compare with the power that is in Christ alone. Those words stand as a constant reminder to flag-wavers of every nation and time.

But Paul also made a small correction that bore directly on the perspective of the liberals. He inserted a single word into the formula favored by the Hellenistic Christians. He added "holiness" to the phrase "according to the spirit," making it into the odd expression we now have in the Romans creed: "according to the spirit *of holiness*." This is the only time this phrase appears in the Old or New Testaments, and its precise interpretation has been a bone of contention among exegetes for generations. The oddity of this expression is an indication to scholars of editorial activity, because the normal antithesis as we observed earlier was simply "according to the flesh vs. according to the spirit."

Paul's use of this term *holiness* in other locations provides a clear indication of what he had in mind with his subtle editing. The liberal Christians of the early church who

31

boasted of being in the spirit often felt it was irrelevant to submit to the norm of moral holiness. They felt freed from the bonds of class and creed, released from the expectations and ambitions of the larger society. Like modern Christians who have undergone dramatic conversion experiences, the spirit set them free from a variety of hangups, both social and moral. With spirit came freedom, and with freedom came a kind of abandon, a letting go. And this is precisely the danger Paul wished to address by the addition of one little word: "holiness."

The Pauline doctrine of holiness was that those who had accepted Christ as savior and Lord entered thereby into the sphere of divine holiness. The righteousness of God enveloped them, qualifying all their subsequent activities, giving them a new motivation to work for justice and the redemption of the world. To be a Christian thus meant to be sanctified, shaped by the holy righteousness of God. Paul frequently refers to Christians as "saints," persons whose behavior reflects the holiness of God. These ideas were decisive for the Wesleyan movement, embodied in the motto "scriptural holiness," so they are part of the heritage we celebrate and study at Garrett-Evangelical. United Methodists know from long experience that the constant companion of charismatic conversion is antinomianism, that spiritual experience without ethical holiness can become demonic, that those who have thrown off the compulsions of the old nature and have trampled on the flags of their former creeds require a new form of self-control.

This is even more true for seminarians and theologians than for others, because we tend to go the farthest in shredding old flags in the name of the spirit. In our study and worship in a seminary setting, we revel in the antithesis between flesh and spirit, the old world and the new, and thus become peculiarly vulnerable to the flesh. The moral integrity of genuine love is thus a requirement for each one of us. Our theological creeds are useless and even dangerous without practical holiness. Thus the apostle Paul sought to hold it all together, proclaiming Jesus

born of David's seed according to the flesh,
appointed son of God in power according to the spirit of holiness,
through the resurrection from the dead . . . (author's trans.)

So who receives the gold medal in the creedal Olympics? There are many who would say that Paul alone deserves the gold. He took it upon himself to supply the final corrections in the early Christian creed in the first chapter of Romans, so his is surely the ultimate word. I myself have at times been one who would plunge headlong into battle under his banner, sweeping all other considerations aside. Many seminary faculty members in the current and last generation were shaped by neoorthodoxy or evangelicalism, having undergone a theological education whose chief hope was to emerge from years of training with the final definition of the truth, the inside track to the most important gold medal of all. In a sense we all want to become winners, to stand on the victor's platform with misty eyes as our anthem is played.

But that is not what Paul provides in Romans. The creed he cites is a composite, typical of all subsequent creeds. It contains several flags, which, taken by themselves alone, would be thoroughly contradictory. How can Paul quote a nationalistic creed and still accept the colors of an ecumenical faith? How can he support both a conservative and a liberal outlook? How can he allow both an emphasis on radical freedom from the law and a commitment to ethical holiness?

The answer is to be found in the words that introduce and conclude the early Christian confession. The opening words of the creedal section were "the gospel concerning his son" and the closing words were "Jesus Christ our Lord." The

33

frame of the creed is Christ; he comes before it and after it, even though the creed seeks to define him. And although we theologians and ministers have struggled for two thousand years to refine these definitions adequately, there is a very real sense in which Christ transcends our best efforts. In theology, we work with refracted light—the pure light of divine truth that constantly shines upon us, glowing in our hearts by faith as we come to know Christ more intimately. But the source of that refracted light cannot be gazed upon with naked eye lest we humans be blinded by glory. We are called to do our best to define and to live up to the small spectrum of truth that has been entrusted to us, but we are never to confuse that spectrum with the divine source itself.[5]

We live by creeds shaped by mortals who have responded to the light in the past, but they always need correction and updating and restating in language our people understand. In contrast to the Olympics, however, there are no particular winners in the Christian race. Alongside Paul there are John and Matthew and Peter. They and we are all gold medalists, standing by grace in the light that Christ has shed out of love for a darkened world.

For this reason, we share a common loaf in our communion services, and drink from a common cup. The Christ who gave himself in the Last Supper died for others rather than defeat them. By placing himself last, he made all of us first. His lordship both incorporates and transcends all of our creeds and flags. Although the best an Olympic competition can do is to determine a temporary winner, Christ unites us in a new fellowship in which each is equal and each is beloved. This provides the abiding center of genuine cross-cultural ministry.

It seems to me that the world was given a spectacular embodiment of ecumenical unity arising from conflict in the Seoul Olympic Games. The opening ceremony featured two teams of more than eleven hundred participants playing the

34

Cha Chun Game. Each team had a huge woven rope shaped like a dragon's head and body, carried by square columns of white-uniformed men with long poles on their shoulders. Dragon flags were carried by the men riding on top of the rope dragon, and long waving tails of red-costumed and blue-costumed dancers followed along behind. These fearsome dragons echoed the symbolism of vulnerability in nightmares and fairy tales throughout the world. This Korean village game probably originated as a military exercise of some kind whose goal was to overthrow the enemies' dragon.

The first time the two teams crashed into each other, the gigantic dragons went high up into the air, and it seemed that the men on top were struggling for ascendancy. But the second time they met and heaved into the sky, the competitive captains put their arms around each other and exchanged their blue and red flags. The two teams then backed away and went out of the arena side by side, their drummer teams playing in unison, and their weaving tails forming a kind of rainbow. The Korean announcer said, "Conflict is transformed into harmony."

This oriental vision of the union of the blue and the red, the yin and the yang, the female and the male principles, the earth and the sky, is consistent with the symbolism of the South Korean national flag. But it also seems to embody the vision of the full spectrum of colors in the early Christian creed. There are no bronze or silver medals in the Creedal Olympics. As we serve in the church of Jesus Christ, we are each called on to display our multicolored banners with boldness and humility, knowing that we are all accepted unconditionally by grace. We should therefore unite with one voice of praise and thanksgiving as we declare together this ancient confession,

the gospel concerning his son, "born of David's seed according to the flesh, appointed son of God in power according to the spirit of holiness, through the resurrection from the dead," Jesus Christ our Lord, through whom we have received grace . . . Amen. (author's trans.)

Notes

1. The rhetorical structure of this passage is discussed by Johannes Weiss, "Beiträge zur Paulinischen Rhetorik," in C. R. Gregory, et al., eds., *Theologische Studien: Herrn Professor D. Bernhard Weiss zu seinem 70 Geburtstage dargebracht* (Gottingen: Vandenhoeck & Ruprecht, 1897), p. 211; and J. P. Louw, *A Semantic Discourse Analysis of Romans* (Pretoria: University of Pretoria), p. 34.
2. See Frank M. Oppenheim, S.J., *Royce's Mature Philosophy of Religion* (Notre Dame: University of Notre Dame Press, 1987).
3. See the articles by Wolfgang Wiefel, Francis Watson, Peter Lampe, and Robert Jewett in Karl Paul Donfried, ed., *The Romans Debate*, rev. and expanded ed. (Peabody, Mass.: Hendrickson, 1991); and Robert Jewett, *Romans* (Nashville: United Methodist Publishing, 1988).
4. See Robert Jewett, "The Redaction and Use of an Early Christian Confession in Romans 1:3-4," pp. 99-122, in D. E. Groh and R. Jewett, eds., *The Living Bible Text: Essays in Honor of Earnest W. Saunders* (Lanham, Md.: University Press of America, 1985); and James D. G. Dunn, *Romans 1–8* (Dallas: Word, 1988), pp. 5-16.
5. See Robert Jewett, *Christian Tolerance: Paul's Message to the Modern Church* (Philadelphia: Westminster Press, 1982), pp. 68-91.

CHAPTER TWO

Feminist Theology in Global Context

—Rosemary Radford Ruether

Rosemary Radford Ruether holds an M.A. and a Ph.D. from Claremont Graduate School in the fields of Classics and Patristics. She is a Catholic feminist theologian and is the Georgia Harkness Professor of Applied Theology at G-ETS and a member of the Graduate Faculty in the Joint Program of Religious and Theological Studies of Northwestern University in Evanston, Illinois. Dr. Ruether has written or edited twenty-two books in the areas of theology and social justice, particularly in the areas of feminism, war and peace, Third World liberation theology, and Jewish-Christian and Palestinian relationships. She is also a regular writer for many Christian periodicals.

In recent years Dr. Ruether has taken a particular interest in the development of feminist theology among Third World women. She has visited several countries in Central America, as well as Mexico, South Africa, Korea, Japan, India, Egypt, and Israel, as part of her dialogue with the development of feminist theology and women's studies among women in Africa, Asia, Latin America, and the Middle East. She is in regular communication with women who are working on these issues in these countries, as well as other countries, such as the Philippines. She is also in dialogue with the work being done through the Women's Commission of the Ecumenical Association of Third World Theologians.

In this article, Dr. Ruether summarizes some of the developments of feminist theology among Third World women through the Women's Commission and indicates why it is important for Christians in the West to be aware of and learn from these developments among women in other countries and cultures.

Feminist theology has often been seen as a white Western women's movement, while liberation theology is seen as springing from the anticolonial movements of Latin America, Asia, and Africa. However, increasingly, women from Latin America, Asia, and Africa are discussing what Ghanaian feminist theologian Mercy Amba Oduyoye called "the irruption within the irruption"; that is, the irruption of Third World feminist theologies within liberation theologies.

One of the principal vehicles of dialogue among Third World liberation theologies has been the Ecumenical Association of Third World Theologians (EATWOT). When this association began its meetings in the early 1970s, women were almost entirely absent and liberation theology was still seen as a Latin American phenomenon. But Asian and African theologians were devising their own contextual theologies, seeking to relate Christianity to their own cultures and liberation struggles. The dialogue among Latin American, Asian, and African theologians was not always easy. Asians and Africans insisted that they had to give attention to cultural issues that had not been prominent in Latin American theologies. As minority churches in non-Christian societies, they had to engage in dialogue with the older Asian and African religions and cultures.

Toward the mid 1970s a few women, such as Mercy Amba Oduyoye, now Deputy General Secretary of the World Council of Churches, began to appear at EATWOT meetings and to point out the need to take women and women's issues seriously within liberation theologies. There was resistance to feminist issues from Third World male theologians. It was said that feminism was a first world issue, that feminism was not an issue in Third World liberation struggles, that the issue of feminism was foreign to Third World cultures. But the women disagreed and began to ask for a women's commission within EATWOT.

In 1983, EATWOT met in Geneva in a joint meeting with European and North American theologians concerned with liberation theology. The meeting was organized so that the delegations from each of the five regions would be as close to 50 percent women as possible. At this meeting, which I attended, the women of all five regions gravitated to one another and claimed their right to meet together on women's issues, despite the protests of some Third World men, who tried to bring "their women" back in line.

At the conclusion of the conference, the women from Asia, Africa, and Latin America stood up together and declared that "feminism is our issue, and we will define what it means for us. It is not for first world women to define it for us, nor is it for third world men to tell us it is not our issue." As Mercy Oduyoye and Virginia Fabella, a Filipina and Asia Coordinator of EATWOT, put it in the book they edited, *With Passion and Compassion: Third World Women Doing Theology* (Orbis Books, 1988),

> We, the women of the Association, were just as concerned to name the demons and to have them exorcised. Sexism was one such demon, and it existed within the Association itself. Our voices were not being heard, although we were visible enough. It became clear to us that only the oppressed can truly name their oppression. We demanded to be heard. The result was the creation within EATWOT of a Women's Commission, and not a Commission of Women as some of the male members would have it. Rather than see ourselves solely as victims of male domination, we formed a sisterhood of resistance to all forms of oppression, seeking creative partnership with men of the Association. (pp. ix-x)

39

Over the next five years, a series of assemblies on Third World feminist theology took place through the organizational initiatives of the Women's Commission of EATWOT. The assemblies were planned to take place in four stages: first, national meetings, then continental and regional meetings, then a Third World global meeting. Finally there would be a global meeting of Third World women theologians with first world women theologians (scheduled for 1990). The continental or regional meetings took place in late 1985 and early 1986. The all-Asian meeting assembled in Manila and the Latin American meeting in Buenos Aires. There were two African meetings, an Anglophone gathering in Port Harcourt, Nigeria, and a Francophone meeting in Yaounde, Cameroun. During December 1–6, 1986, delegations from these three regions met together at Oaxtepec, Mexico.

These meetings stimulated continuing networks nationally and regionally, as well as a flow of publications. The resolutions from the Asian, the Latin American, and the two African assemblies, together with the resolutions from the global meeting, were published, along with important presentations, in the book edited by Fabella and Oduyoye already mentioned. The Latin American papers also were published in a book edited by Mexican New Testament scholar, Elsa Tamez, *El Rostro Femenino de la Teologia* (1986), English translation *Through Her Eyes: Women's Theology from Latin America* (Orbis Books, 1989).

Asian women have become particularly active, with national groups continuing on in several countries, especially Korea, India, and the Philippines. They have founded the Asian Women's Resource Center, located in Hong Kong. Book publications and a quarterly journal, *In God's Image*, edited by Korean feminist theologian Sun Ai Park, emanate from this center. Drawing from papers from regional meetings, the Resource Center has published *We Dare to Dream: Doing Theology as Asian Women* (1989), reprinted by Orbis Books. Asian feminist theologians continue to organize gatherings, such as the assembly at Singapore, November 1987. Its papers were published by the Resource Center under the title *Asian Women Doing Theology* (1989). What are the distinctive issues of Third World feminist theology? How do feminist religious leaders from such diverse regions as Brazil and Mexico, India, Korea, and the Philippines, and Ghana, Nigeria, Cameroun, and South Africa contextualize feminist reflection in their ecclesial, social, and cultural situations? Despite this enormous diversity, there are many similarities between feminist writings on Christology, God-language, or church and ministry coming from these many regions.

This similarity reflects the fact that these women are Christians who have received their Christianity from Western European and North American missionaries. These women have also been educated in a Western European or North American Catholic or Protestant culture. Their languages of communication came to them from the missionaries and colonialists, Spanish or Portuguese, French or English. In order to become Christians they or their ancestors were uprooted from their indigenous cultures and religions. They all share some similar problems that come from this history of cultural and socioeconomic colonialism and its contemporary realities of neocolonial dependency and exploitation.

One can analyze several aspects of Third World women's development of feminist theology. One aspect is the appropriation of feminist theology and social analysis that has appeared in North America and Western Europe. Anglophone women in Africa and Asia might read materials from North America, while Latin Americans often also draw on French feminism. But Third World women are often multilingual. Korean feminists, for example, are also well aware of German, as well as American, feminism.

Much of the critique of patriarchalism in the church and in

society that has been undertaken in the West is quite relevant for these Third World women, because this same patriarchalism has been exported by the West to Latin America, Asia, and Africa. Women in Mexico, or in India or in Korea or in Nigeria or in South Africa, find themselves confronted with colonialist and missionary versions of patriarchal economic and political patterns and male clericalism. They hear versions of the same biblical and theological arguments declaring that God has created male headship and forbidden women to be ordained. Thus, for example, when a Korean woman undertakes feminist New Testament exegesis, drawing on the work of Elisabeth Schüssler Fiorenza, she has in mind, not simply a patriarchal biblical interpretation in the West, but one she has had to confront in her own church and theological school.

A second aspect of Third World feminist reflection relates to social analysis. Third World women begin to tell their own stories and reclaim their own histories as Korean women, as Mexican women, as Khosa women in South Africa, or as Filipinas. Here the stories become more diverse and distinctive, although the patterns are similar. For most of these Third World women, there is a keen interest in the status of women in their native culture before colonialization. For example, Mexican anthropologist Sylvia Marcos has researched the roles of women in healing within the cosmovision of Meso-American cultures prior to their shattering by Spanish colonialism (*Trabajo, Poder y Sexualidad,* Colegio de Mexico, 1989). Filipina scholar, Sister Mary John Mananzan, has written on similar changes in Polynesian society, brought about by the Spanish colonialism in the Philippines (*Essays on Women,* Manila, 1987; and *Women and Religion,* Manila, 1988).

The storytelling of Third World women also includes their current stories, how their socialization by Christian and Western cultures has made them feel about themselves as Asians or Africans and as women. Middle-class women reach

42

out to poor women and create gatherings where these women can tell their stories of poverty and sexual exploitation. Out of these stories Third World women devise a social analysis of the issues of women in their context. They move beyond a middle-class feminism of "equality" to a liberation feminism, locating gender oppression in relation to the structure of class and racial oppression. Solidarity with the oppressed and preferential option for the poor take on an additional and more specific focus. It comes to mean solidarity with these oppressed and exploited poor women of their own countries. These are the poorest of the poor, the *minjung* of the *minjung*, to use the terminology of Korean liberation feminism.

Sexual exploitation of women cuts across class lines. There is rape or incest of the female child in the home, wife battering, rape in the streets, and denial of reproductive decision making for the middle-class women, as well as the poor woman. All women bear the burden of sexual stereotyping and domestic labor. But these burdens are aggravated for poor women by poverty. The wealthy woman can employ the poor woman to alleviate her work in housecleaning and childcare, while the poor woman has to neglect her own children to labor for poor wages and in exploitative conditions in the houses of the rich. The poor woman also faces the dangers of the streets, where she may be robbed and raped, or the oppression and health hazards of the factory, as she tries to earn money to support the children she may have had to leave unattended at home.

In their gatherings, Third World women share the historically specific aspects of social, economic, and political oppression in their countries and how these affect the oppression of women. Discussion of women's oppression also brings out specific cultural problems. For example, in India an important focus of feminist organizing has been in behalf of the tens of thousands of Indian women who have died or been severely injured in dowry murders or attempted murders. The dowry has become a way of exploiting the economic relation of the bride's to the groom's family. The low view of the woman as an expendable commodity, to be valued only for the goods she brings with her, is greatly exaggerated under the influence of Western consumerism. The groom's family demands a large sum of money and expensive consumer goods as the price for taking the bride into their family. Once these goods are delivered, together with the hapless bride, kitchen accidents are contrived to burn her to death. The groom and his family then go looking for another bride (see *In God's Image*, September 1989).

For Korean feminists, the forcible division of their country into two parts after the Second World War, North and South, capitalist and communist, each repressively a bad example of the two antagonistic world systems on which they depend, has become the focus for feminist theological reflection. Korean feminists have widened the scope of this analysis to include other antagonistic dualisms within Korean society— urban and rural, rich and poor, and, especially, male-female hierarchy, with its rigid construction by Confucian social ideology. They have suggested that all these antagonistic dualisms are merely various expressions of the one foundational paradigm of patriarchy. To be liberated, the Korean people must overcome all these antagonistic dualisms, not by setting one side against the other, but by transcending the dualistic antagonisms in a new harmonious synthesis (see *In God's Image*, June 1988).

Another difficult issue for Third World feminists is cultural pluralism, particularly in relation to indigenous religions and cultures that persist underneath Western Christian colonialism. Indigenous or culturally contextual theologies, such as African theology, have sought to appropriate for Christianity positive traits of traditional religions (see Kofi Appiah-Kubi and Sergio Torres, *Theology of Liberation*, Orbis Books, 1988).

44

But sometimes such appropriation of indigenous religions and cultures by Christians is romantic and unhistorical. It treats such cultures as static and unchanging and ignores negative aspects. For feminists in Asia and Africa, such indigenous theologies have been problematic in their failure to recognize the elements in the traditional culture that are oppressive to women. Many feminists in countries where the indigenous religion and culture are still strong have concluded that they suffer from doubled layers of patriarchal domination.

Christianity, instead of liberating women, has become a tool to reenforce the patriarchalism of the traditional culture. For example, in India Christianity is used to reenforce traditional Hindu restrictions on women. In Korea a Christian emphasis on the family is used to reenforce a Confucian view of the patriarchal family (see Nation Papers from India, Indonesia, Japan, and Korea, in *In God's Image*, September 1987).

Third World women also find positive resources for feminism in some aspects of indigenous religion and culture. Some Korean women have found helpful resources in Shamanism, where women predominate (see Chung Hyun Kyung, "Han pu-ri: Doing Theology from Korean Women's Perspective," in *We Dare to Dream*, 135-46). They also claim the liberating traditions of Christianity as a basis for Christian feminism, even as they protest the failure of the Christian churches to recognize this message.

The relation of Third World women to the plurality of their cultural heritages must be complex and dialectical, rather than one of simplistic dualism. Instead of repudiating either culture in the name of an idealized view of the other, they wish to excise the patriarchal elements from both cultures and bring the liberating elements of Christianity together with the holistic elements of indigenous culture. Third World feminists face staggering difficulties of cultural and social oppression, but the promise of their creative vision is very great.

45

CHAPTER THREE

Recent Religious Developments: A New Testament Theological Perspective

—W. Richard Stegner

As a result of the establishment of the Center for Asian-American Ministries, there has been a dramatic increase in the number of Asian students in the various degree programs of Garrett-Evangelical Theological Seminary. How does this growing Asian presence illustrate the theme of this book: Identifying and Communicating God's Presence in the Cross-Cultural Context? In the following article, W. Richard Stegner seeks to answer that question by placing the growing Asian presence on campus within the context of the rapid growth of the church in the Third World and particularly in Asia. Dr. Stegner finds that the explanations advanced by the secular media for such recent religious developments are not adequate. Rather, he turns to biblical passages and New Testament theology as articulated by the late Oscar Cullmann. The rapid growth of the church in Third World and formerly Communist countries illustrates the continuing work of God in history.

Holding a B.A. from the University of Cincinnati, a B.D. and Ph.D. from Drew University, and with further study experience in Jerusalem and Oxford, Dr. Stegner is currently Professor of New Testament at G-ETS. He has been advising Asian students at G-ETS for the past six years.

Unprecedented political and social changes have taken place since the last few months of 1989. With amazing speed and ease citizens have toppled long-entrenched Communist regimes in Eastern Europe.

Dramatic economic and political changes continue to take place within the former Soviet Union itself. Democracy has come to Panama and Nicaragua.

Unprecedented Religious Developments

At the same time, unprecedented religious developments have also taken place. For example, the recent meeting between the pope and a Russian Communist president was a first. In Eastern Europe state television has aired religious programs. More than one hundred thousand Bulgarians gathered for mass in the central square in Sofia on Christmas Eve. The newly inaugurated Czechoslovakian government attended mass at the cathedral as part of the ceremonies. Hundreds of Russian Orthodox churches have been re-opened, and the churches are crowded.

The news from Communist China is equally dramatic. The church is alive and well and growing in Communist China. The churches in the capital were jammed for Christmas services. "Believers, curiosity seekers and amiable soldiers jammed the capital's lit-up churches, which all miraculously survived centuries of rebellions, wars, official atheism and dogged persecution."[1] Similar developments are reported in Shanghai, where the cathedral has been reopened. The Catholic church claims 120,000 faithful and 36 places of worship in Shanghai alone.

Who are these faithful in Communist China? Father Joseph, the aged priest in charge of the cathedral, reports: "I am not amazed that the young come to church. . . . Most are members of old Christian families where mothers and grandmothers passed on the faith. Now the faith is bearing fruit. The young suffer from a crisis of confidence, they want something to believe in."[2]

The same article that quotes Father Joseph and reports the revival of religion in China also accounts for that revival with

47

the headline "Chinese try religion to fill ideological void." Perhaps a more insightful headline would account for the packed churches on the basis of the cessation of Communist persecution. At any rate, the headline speaks a partial truth. As Father Joseph points out, the young do want something to believe in. The collapse of the Communist world view and program for salvation has left an ideological void. However, the secular reasoning of the headline is not a complete answer.

In order to fill an ideological void, religion had to be present as a live alternative. In short, the secular reasoning of the headline fails to account for the amazing staying power of religious faith in a hostile environment. Again, Father Joseph's answer points in the right direction. He speaks of "old Christian families" whose "mothers and grandmothers passed on the faith." Also, the Orthodox Church in Russia has shown the amazing staying power of the faith in defiance of some of the bloodiest persecutions on record. During seventy years of persistent persecution by an atheistic state, the faith was passed on and constitutes a live option for filling the ideological void caused by the collapse of Communism.

The partial secular answer that religious faith rushes in to fill an ideological void is deficient on other grounds as well. It does not account for the dramatic growth of the faith in areas where there was no ideological void left by Communism. Of course, the rapid growth of the church in places like South Korea and Africa south of the Sahara immediately comes to mind. According to recent estimates, one in four South Koreans is a Christian. Our Methodist membership in South Korea is a good barometer. A few years ago Methodist membership surpassed the one million mark. The church has set a goal of two million members by the year 2000, and the possibility that it will meet that goal is strong. In addition, South Korea has ceased to be a missionary-importing country

48

and has become a missionary-exporting country. South Korea is now sending missionaries to other Asian countries.

At a recent church supper, the Anglican rector and I were lamenting the low state of the church in England. In contrast to England, the rector pointed out that the picture was much more encouraging in places like Africa. Today there are more Anglicans in Africa than there are in England! I contributed that certain Methodist conferences in Africa were establishing new congregations more rapidly than ministers were being trained to fill those pulpits. A priest seated nearby said that of all the missionary provinces in the Roman church, Africa was near the top of the list in winning new converts to Christ.

Finally, the facile secular assumption concerning an ideological void is confounded by Poland. One wit put it this way: In the days of Polish independence, the country imported priests and exported grain, but under Communist control the country exported priests and imported grain! Poland did not experience an ideological void, and the church has gone from strength to strength under the very shadow of the Communist state.

The Paralysis of Contemporary Analysis

Where have we come in our analysis? So far we have commented on the recent religious revival in Russia, in China, and in some Eastern European countries. We have noted the rapid growth of the church in places like South Korea and Africa south of the Sahara. Also, we have argued that the secular interpretation of such developments—that religion fills the ideological void created by the demise of Communism—is only partially adequate. Although it accounts in part for the crowded churches in Russia and China, it does not account for the staying power of faith in those same

49

places. Nor does it account for the recent rapid growth of the church in Third World countries.

Indeed, recent religious developments are a phenomenon that cries out for an explanation. Yet, recent interpreters of religion have turned out to be false prophets. Did not Harvey Cox once predict that ours would be the last generation to worship in churches? Nevertheless, the church is alive and well and experiencing remarkable growth in the least expected places. Did not a death-of-God theology just a few years ago write God's obituary? Yet, Who has buried whom? Truly, God has confounded the wisdom of the wise.

Where, then, shall we look for an explanation? Our secular experts and media have been weighed and found wanting. Shall we turn to sociological analysis? Shall we consult biblical passages for guidance? Dare we say that God is doing a new thing in the world today?

Before we continue with our analysis, a word of caution is in order. Let us not "buy into" the secular option that lies so close at hand. Let us not think that the alternatives are either political and social analysis *or* biblical passages that speak about the work of God. Secular analysis, if it speaks of God at all, would confine religion to the sphere of the private, to the individual conscience. Consequently, some politicians manage the remarkable feat of being both pro-choice and anti-abortion at the same time: They are pro-life as private individuals, but pro-choice for public policy. Hence, religion is another ideology that fills the void in private life when the former ideology collapses. The primary distinction between the two ideologies is that governments, espousing the secular, have the right to dictate public policy whereas religion does not. Let us not allow such secular reasoning to confuse our analysis.

Such a private view of religion is contrary to Scripture as well as traditional Christianity. The Bible claims that God is the Lord of history. If no sparrow falls without his notice,

50

neither does a great empire. For example, the prophet tells us that God called Cyrus, who did not know him, to end the Babylonian captivity of Israel. "For the sake of my servant Jacob, / and Israel my chosen, / I call you by your name, / I surname you, though you do not know me" (Isa. 45:4). "I have aroused Cyrus in righteousness, / . . . he shall build my city / and set my exiles free / . . . says the Lord of hosts" (Isa. 45:13). Accordingly, God works in, under, and through the political and social dimensions of life, as well as in the private sphere. Biblical religion and its Marxist persecutors clearly understand the public nature of religion. Existentialism and its successor, secularism, have tried to confine faith to the private sphere of the individual conscience.

If Isaiah was correct in describing God's preparation for the mission of Cyrus in destroying the Babylonian Empire and subsequently in releasing the exiles, what shall we say about the collapse of the Communist ideology and subsequent growth of the church? Would not a modern Isaiah (if such public revelation were still possible) see the activity of God in the right political, social, and ideological conditions for the renewal and growth of the church? If Nahum could see the judgment of God in the demise of Nineveh, that wicked city, could not a modern Nahum see the judgment of God on an ideology that championed the most hideous violations of human rights and human life? After all, the altars of Communism are running red with the blood of millions of innocent victims, from the Kulaks of the Ukraine to the best of the Polish officer corps in Katyn forest.

A New Testament Theological Perspective

With such an understanding of the activity of God, let us see what light New Testament passages may shed on the current religious revival. In a remarkable essay entitled "The Work of God Goes On," Gerhard Lohfink analyzes the "work" that God does according to the book of Acts.[3] Lohfink quotes, for example, the words of the famous Gamaliel to the earliest persecutors of the church. Let us describe the scene. Shortly after Pentecost, Peter and the apostles are teaching and preaching the Resurrection in Jerusalem. The high priest and the council, having previously arrested Peter and the apostles, this time want to kill them. Gamaliel, a member of the council, gives this advice: "I tell you, keep away from these men and let them alone; because if this plan or this undertaking [*this work* in Greek] is of human origin, it will fail; but if it is of God, you will not be able to overthrow them—in that case you may even be found fighting against God!" (Acts 5:38-39). According to this passage and others, the founding and growth of the church is the work of God. This work of God continues after Easter in the life and mission of the church. If this is true, then God "works" in, under, and through the social and psychological dynamics of life: How else does the call of God come to people? Also, in the sense that the church is a historical phenomenon, the work of God takes place in history.

Perhaps we can add even more specificity to the work of God through the church by examining a remarkable passage in Paul's epistle to the Romans. In chapters 9–11, Paul is discussing the relationship of the church to Israel. As Paul approaches the climax of his argument, he writes this remarkable sentence: "I want you to understand this mystery: a hardening has come upon part of Israel, until the full number of the Gentiles has come in. And so all Israel will be saved" (11:25-26). Though nearly every word in the sentence needs explanation, for our purposes we will discuss only a few of them.

Let us begin with the word *mystery*. The background of this term clarifies its meaning. The background is Jewish and, more specifically, Jewish Apocalyptic, which is both a literary form (i.e., genre) and a way of thinking. Jewish Apocalyptic portrayed God's purposes for history and the nearness of the end, often by means of visions and heavenly journeys. Accordingly, the term "mystery" designates a purpose or secret of God that cannot be known by reason: God must reveal it to selected humans.[4]

According to some apocalyptic speculation, God planned to convert Gentiles to Judaism in the last days. This kind of thinking seems to lie immediately behind Romans 11:25. However, in the "mystery" that Paul is sharing, God has formed a new people in Christ, and the unbelief of the Jewish people has caused the gospel to be preached to the Gentiles. In the end time "all Israel," that is, the Jewish people who do not yet believe in Christ, will be drawn to faith in him by God.

Many interpreters believe that here Paul is sharing "a new special revelation which he has himself received."[5] Others doubt this. Whether or not Paul is speaking about his own experience, God has revealed this insight to a chosen human.

The words translated *the full number of the Gentiles* could more literally be translated "the fullness of the Gentiles." Unfortunately, the meaning of "full number" or "fullness" cannot be described with the same precision as the meaning of the word *mystery*, since Paul does not define it further. As background he probably had in mind the contemporary Jewish teaching that in the end time the nations would be converted and make a pilgrimage to Jerusalem. Also, there seem to be three main possibilities for understanding the word. It can mean "the full number of the elect from among the Gentiles," or "the added number needed in order to make up that full total," or, even, "the Gentile world as a whole."[6]

A Chinese student at G-ETS takes the latter view and speaks eloquently of the need to evangelize more than one billion of his fellow countrypeople. Whether or not he is correct in interpreting "full number" to mean the great majority of the Gentiles, he seems to be correct in insisting that the evangelization of the Gentiles must take place within history. That is, Paul is not speaking of an act of God at the end of this age: He is speaking of the mission of the church. The evidence for this view lies in the words *"come in."* The Greek for "come in" is found only three times elsewhere in Paul, but is frequently used in the Gospels for entering into the kingdom of God. The coming in or entering into the Kingdom took place within Jesus' ministry and takes place today. In using this term, Paul is probably "drawing here on pre-Pauline tradition which stems from Jesus."[7] Thus, Paul seems to have in mind the very kind of evangelistic work in which he himself was engaged when he wrote the letter to the Romans.

Note the precision that this passage from Paul adds to Lohfink's discussion of the work of God. The incoming of the Gentiles takes place in the course of history and is being realized in the growth of the church. In one sense we are witnessing the filling of an ideological vacuum; in another sense we are witnessing the continuing work of God in history. In still another, the fullness of the Gentiles is being realized and God is working out his purpose for history.

The work of God through the church is set within the context of God's redemptive purpose for humanity by Oscar Cullmann, the noted representative of the Salvation History approach to New Testament theology. Among a variety of approaches to New Testament theology, Cullmann's seems most accurately to reflect that of the majority of New Testament writers themselves.

However, before describing the theological framework in which Cullmann places the work of the church, a brief assessment of the criticism of Cullmann's approach is in order, for Cullmann's work has been subjected to intense and hostile criticism for more than forty years. Critics have called into question many of his assertions. In particular, they have shown that Cullmann overemphasized the unity of the New Testament. Rather, there was theological and ethnic diversity in the church almost from the beginning. For example, Cullmann could hardly have foreseen the current interest in Jewish Christianity and its theology. Only recently have new critical methodologies opened that door. On the other hand, the New Testament does contain unifying themes and trajectories: It is more than a collection of divers and different theologies. Certainly, one source of unity of the New Testament is the apocalyptic world view most New Testament writers presupposed.

The apocalyptic world view presupposes that God has a purpose for history and that God is working that purpose out in history. History is moving toward eschatological promise and salvation. Accordingly, Cullmann's linear concept of time (history is going somewhere) is quite compatible with apocalyptic thought. Although Cullmann's concept of time may not be found in every New Testament book, it is found in most. Most New Testament writings picture the church as living between advents, between the already and the not yet, between the initial inbreaking of God's Kingdom in Jesus and its full coming at the end of history. Also, the concept of resurrection belongs to the apocalyptic world view. Thus, there is considerable overlap between the apocalyptic world view and Cullmann's approach to New Testament theology. Again, the current interest in apocalyptic arose after Cullmann made his chief contributions.

Whether or not the apocalyptic world view is adequate for the church of today is very much a matter of debate, but this debate cannot be pursued here. Suffice it to say that in my view an apocalyptic world view is in some sense normative.

How does Cullmann set the work of the church within the context of redemptive history? What is Cullmann's approach? The title of Cullmann's well-known book, *Christ and Time: The Primitive Christian Conception of Time and*

History, contains his basic thesis.[8] The New Testament writers, as well as the Old Testament prophets, held a linear conception of time in contrast to others who view time either as cyclical or as illusory. Because time is linear, history also has a beginning, middle, and end. However, there is a particular history in which God chooses to reveal himself: namely, the history of the Jews. The very midpoint of this history is the Christ-event, where God reveals himself most fully. The primary focus of the Christ-event is his death and resurrection. It is the midpoint in that the sacrificial death of Jesus atones for the sin of the world, and the resurrection of Jesus gives hope to our lives here and hope for life after death.

The midpoint, where God's rule (Kingdom) breaks into our time, points to the end of history when God's rule will be fully realized. In describing the relationship of the Christ-event at the midpoint to the full coming of God's rule at the end of history, Cullmann uses an analogy drawn from World War II. He speaks of the Christ-event as D-Day and the fullness of God's rule at the end of the historical drama as V-Day. D-Day stands for the decisive battle in a war, and V-Day stands for victory day when the war is won and is over. After the Allies had established a second front in Normandy and the Germans were not able to push them back into the sea, everyone knew the decisive battle had been fought: It was just a matter of time until Germany, now fighting on two fronts, would have to surrender. Similarly, Christ's death and resurrection is the decisive battle fought against sin, death, and the devil. The decisive battle points to God's final victory in the full coming of his rule at the end of history. Then, all ambiguities and suffering will meet their fulfillment in the kingdom of God.

The church is located on the time line between D-Day and V-Day: This time span is "the period of the Church."[9] In World War II, many fierce battles were fought after D-Day. If the decisive battle has been fought at Calvary and won in the Resurrection, what further battles must be fought and won before V-Day? The church battles sin, death, and the devil through its proclamation of God's decisive victory in the Christ-event at the midpoint. Cullmann makes this crystal clear. "This missionary proclamation of the Church, its preaching of the gospel, gives to the period between Christ's resurrection and Parousia its meaning for redemptive history."[10] Paul gives the same message in Romans 10:17: "So faith comes from what is heard, and what is heard comes through the word of [about] Christ." Thus, successive battles are won as increasing numbers come to faith in Jesus.

However, after D-Day there were also setbacks and losses, such as the Battle of the Bulge in Belgium. In like manner, the church has seemed to suffer one defeat after another at the hands of atheistic Communism, which did bestride the earth like a colossus. But this idol too had feet of clay and fell. The words of Revelation 14:8 seem a fitting epitaph: "Fallen, fallen is Babylon the great! She [who] made all nations drink of the wine of the wrath of her fornication." The poet John Bowring put it this way: "In the cross of Christ I glory, towering o'er the wrecks of time."

Today, great victories are being won for Jesus. Eager young Asians, Africans, and other Third World peoples are enlisting. And South Korea has become a missionary-exporting nation. The work of God goes on until V-Day, until the full number of Gentiles have come in.

Notes

1. *Chicago Tribune*, Monday, 25 December 1989, p. 32.
2. *Chicago Tribune*, Thursday, 2 November 1989, p. 27.
3. Gerhard Lohfink, *The Work of God Goes On*, The Bible for Christian Life Series (Philadelphia: Fortress Press, 1987), pp. 13-27.
4. C. E. B. Cranfield, *A Critical and Exegetical Commentary on the Epistle to the Romans*, I.C.C. (Edinburgh: T. and T. Clark, 1979), p. 574.
5. Ibid., p. 573.
6. Ibid., pp. 575-76.

7. James D. G. Dunn, *Romans 9–16*, Word Biblical Commentary, vol. 38 (Waco, Tex.: Word, 1988), p. 680.
8. Oscar Cullmann, *Christ and Time: The Primitive Christian Conception of Time and History*, rev. ed. (Philadelphia: Westminster Press, n.d.).
9. Ibid., p. 150.
10. Ibid., p. 157.

PART TWO:
ATTITUDE

CHAPTER FOUR

Strangers and Foreigners

—James B. Ashbrook

*In his piece "Strangers and Foreigners," James B. Ashbrook
writes about the life of faith as it is experienced by emigrants
and immigrants. Using Abraham and Sarah as a special
example of faithfulness, he explores migration in whatever
form as a clue to what faith is about. We are all called by God
to leave our pasts for the sake of God's future. We are all
called by God to travel without road maps and guidebooks,
continually risking all in a readiness to respond. Life in "the
Promised Land" is never easy, because we can never settle
down as though we were at home. As people of faith, we are a
people-on-the-move, upsetting every status quo and going
beyond every established authority. We look toward God's
surprising and unexpected future with confidence because we
can look to Jesus as God's offspring, the pioneer and perfecter
of our faith.*

*This article suggests that we are all immigrants and all live
within that cross-cultural context. The knowledge provided
through this sermon should help us to nurture an attitude of
openness toward the diversity of cultures in our society.*

*Though not an immigrant himself, Dr. Ashbrook has pulled
up the stakes of his life in responding to God's leading from
parish pastor to seminary professor, from an American
Baptist seminary to a United Methodist seminary, and from
one part of the United States to another. Dr. Ashbrook
received a Ph.D. from Ohio State University and an LL.D.
from Denison University. He is currently Professor of
Religion and Personality at Garrett-Evangelical Theological*

61

Seminary. His recent contributions to scholarship and church include The Brain and Belief: Faith in the Light of Brain Research *and* Paul Tillich in Conversation, *and the development of a model for integrating religious resources and clinical functioning in pastoral counseling and psychotherapy.*

Let us explore together the meaning of being an emigrant people in this land in which many are immigrants. Although I am not an immigrant, my faith is the emigrant faith of the Bible, and so it is that faith which I explore with you in this meditation.

The powerful words of the book of Hebrews describe the lives of us all: "Not having received what was promised, but having seen it and greeted it from afar." Then the writer goes on to put in even sharper focus our experience of struggling to live:

> and having acknowledged that they were strangers and exiles on the earth. For people who speak thus make it clear that they are seeking a homeland. If they had been thinking of that land from which they had gone out, they would have had opportunity to return. But as it is, they desire a better country, that is, a heavenly one. Therefore God is not ashamed to be called their God, for he has prepared for them a city . . . whose builder and maker is God. (11:13-16, 10)

More than any other people, those who are immigrants know what it's like to be strangers and exiles. The uprooting of their lives in hopes of finding a truer home, a heavenly one, is more real to them than to one like myself who is at home and is a citizen of these United States. Yet whether they are strangers or I am at home, each of us is called by God in faith—like Abraham and Sarah—to go out from the places of our lives "not knowing where we are to go." Whether one is a citizen or an alien, all of us are called by God in faith—like

Abraham and Sarah—"to journey in the land of promise as in a foreign land, living in tents, looking forward to that heavenly place whose builder and maker is God." Whether we dwell in the land of our birth or live in the land of our becoming, both are called by God in faith—like Abraham and Sarah—to that which is ever promised yet never fulfilled. I suggest that those who are literally strangers and immigrants here in the United States have within their own hearts and minds a knowledge of the life of faith, which is God's Word for all humanity.

God calls us all—citizens and aliens alike—to be in this world as strangers. What, then, is it like to be in this world as strangers? How do we live that life of faith in the land of the living? What does it mean to be the people of God? First of all—perhaps most important of all—we are called to travel.

We Are Called to Travel

The story of Abraham and Sarah is not just a story about a couple living in the long ago, packing up and moving from Ur of the Chaldeans across the fertile crescent down into Egypt and then back up into Canaan. No, the story of Abraham and Sarah is the age-old story, the ageless story, the universal story of people of faith. Migration—emigration and immigration—that's what faith is about. To make the journey, we needn't necessarily pack up and leave home. Instead the story tells us that our lives are to be open to God's leading. God calls us to leave the places of our past, to be in the present, for the sake of God's future.

God calls us to become the *human* community, that community in which every person—young and old, rich and poor, male and female, insider and outsider, native and immigrant—is a member of the *whole* family of God. That is our inheritance—inexhaustible humanizing. We are called out to celebrate the goodness of God's making all things new. We are called out to know that every creature is a creation of

63

God. We are called out to accept God's unconditional acceptance of us as we are, that we might become the people God means us to become. We are called out to recognize that we belong to God because God has loved us from the beginning. This is our inheritance; this is our goal; this is our destiny; this is our place; this is our home—the Good News of the gospel of Jesus Christ that there is no life that is not life together in God.

But if, as people of faith, we are called to travel, how do we plan our travel? Where is God taking us? How do we prepare? What do we take? On what can we count?

We Can Count on Uncertainty

Listen to the words of Hebrews again: "By faith Abraham obeyed when he was called to set out for a place that he was to receive as an inheritance; and he set out, not knowing where he was going" (11:8).

When you came to the United States, you had *some* idea of where you were going. You had *some* plan as to what you would do. You had *some* inkling of what would be involved. But in our journey in faith, we have *no* idea where we are going. We have *no* plan as to what we are to do. We have *no* inkling of what will be involved.

Even though we are called to joy in the service of our Lord, we are never certain what we are about. God gives us no road map, no travel plans, no flight schedule, no guidebook with sure directions. Our life in faith is as the great Jewish thinker Martin Buber put it: We who live "must perpetually begin anew, perpetually risk all; and therefore [our] truth is not a having but a becoming."[1] "The person who knows direction responds with the whole of [one's] being to each new situation with no other preparation than [one's] presence and [one's] readiness to respond."[2]

Historians see history as turning points made up of chance

64

and accident and also as the result of deliberate planning. But for people of faith, under and within and beyond all planning, is seen the moving presence of the Almighty One, the "I am who I am," "I will be who I will be," the bestower of inexhaustible humanizing. As people of faith, we claim God is in the midst of our today, even as God was in the midst of our yesterdays and will be there in the midst of our tomorrows. With God every point is a turning point. With God no point is so removed that it cannot lead us directly to God. We do not know where we are going or how we are going or when we are going when we are called to go out of our limited lives for the sake of the larger life in God. In any specific moment we may be uncertain what we are about, yet we are ever certain it is God who is calling us to the responsible life with the whole human family.

Our uncertainty about the trip is ever balanced by our certainty about the One who calls us to go out. But you know better than I know that life in the promised land is never easy.

We Are Never at Home

Listen again to the Scripture: "By faith Abraham obeyed when he was called to set out for a place that he was to receive as an inheritance; and he set out, not knowing where he was going. By faith he stayed for a time in the land he had been promised, as in a foreign land" (Heb. 11:8-9).

Those are hard words—traveling in the land of promise "as in a foreign land." Life is hard. When we are uncertain of what we are being called out to live, we discover only that we are never to be at home. Quite clearly, as people of faith we live where we live as strangers, foreigners, exiles, aliens, outsiders. Even in the place of promise, our place is unfamiliar.

I think the writer is reminding us that life in God is ever at odds with life in the world. No street is ever *our* street, no town is ever *our* town, no region is ever *our* region, no

65

country is ever *our* country. Perhaps even more disconcerting, no church is ever *our* church. We live on the street with our address; we dwell in the town of our choice; we roam in the region around us; we are part of the country where we pay taxes; we rejoice in the church in which we worship—but none of these, not one of these, no not one of them, is the place we are at home.

In faith we are ever in a foreign land, a place that is less than the promised City of God. And more than not being at home, the writer of Hebrews puts the issue of being uprooted even stronger.

We Are to Be Unsettled

Listen again to those ringing words, those relentless words, those words which call us again and again to the life of faith: "By faith Abraham obeyed when he was called to set out for a place that he was to receive as an inheritance; and he set out, not knowing where he was going. By faith he stayed for a time in the land he had been promised, as in a foreign land, living in tents."

"Living in tents"—again the unexpected, again the uncertain, again the uncomfortable, again the uprooted. No settling down, no digging in, no permanent place. In contrast to a building, a tent reminds us of being on the move. A tent is something we put up quickly and take down easily. A tent is something that takes little effort. Our faith reminds us that we are a people on the move.

This unsettledness, however, doesn't necessarily require our actually moving. We must be quite clear about that, even though those of you who emigrate and immigrate have a special understanding of the life of faith. Living in tents is more an attitude of mind and heart than a matter of muscles and motion. It means keeping life open to the fresh winds of the Spirit blowing where it will.

66

In their life in Canaan, the Hebrews experienced the clash between Yahweh and Baalim, the recognized gods of the land. The word *baal* refers to "possessor" or "inhabitant." The baalim, therefore, were the proprietors of various activities, especially the proprietors of particular towns and special places. In effect, they were "immobile gods . . . the gods of a sedentary people who were suspicious of any kind of change" (Harvey Cox).

In contrast, Yahweh is a mobile God. Yahweh frees us from special places. Yahweh wipes out special classes. Yahweh's people travel, for Yahweh sets before us an open road and a beckoning world.

A people on the move assume many forms. It may be as a house church where early in the morning people gather around a breakfast table, discuss their work, share their concerns, break bread, drink wine, and praise God. It may be as a small luncheon in the Chicago Loop, where office workers gather to talk about what is happening to them and how their faith matters in what they are doing. It may be as a picket line singing "Deep in my heart, I do believe, we shall overcome someday." It may be as an inner-city storefront church where the dispossessed know someone listens; someone cares; someone fights for cleaner toilets, fewer rats, better schools, stabler families. It may be as a church mortgaging its property to invest in low-income affordable housing. It may be as a hospital where a nurse unburdens herself to a chaplain her fears of death as she cares for a woman her own age dying of breast cancer.

A people on the move upset every status quo. A people on the move question every established power—whether emperor, pope, prime minister, president, mayor, teacher, pastor, yes, and even parent. A people on the move trigger social change. Wherever life is on the line—in slum or suburb, in industry or education, in hospitals or housing, in Congress or the United Nations, abroad or at home—the power of

67

becoming the people of Yahweh God is ever and always at work. Finally, we never arrive yet always know our home.

We Never Arrive Yet Always Know Our Home

"These all died in faith, not having received what was promised." Unfinished, incomplete, uncertain. We are outsiders even when we are at home, we can never settle down, and now we are reminded that we never receive the promise of our inheritance. What kind of faith is this?

Here we face the strange and wonderful mystery of the people of Yahweh God. A life of faith is open-ended. No matter how much we do, there is still more to be done. No matter what we are, there is still more to become. No matter what happens, unexpected possibilities await us—in God, in faith, in hope, in love. Every moment bears in the womb of time new possibilities.

We can see the promises in the distance. We can hail them as true. We are convinced of their reality. So we travel. We fix our eyes on the genuine human family of God. We long for the fullest and truest life in God, against which our everyday life is both a manifestation and never a realized reality.

It is not easy to maintain the creative tension between being called out *from* the world and being sent *to* the world. We can get so caught up with not being *of* the world that we end up not being *in* the world. On the other hand, we can get so caught up with being *in* the world that we end up being *of* the world.

The vision shows us we are to be in the world as fools—free from pretense, free from fear, free from self-consciousness, free from one another, free to be for and with one another—in ways that matter genuinely. We are to be fools for Christ's sake.

Yes, we have our own private hopes, we make our own private plans, we carry out our own private purpose according to *our own* understanding of God's calling. Yet all our anticipations are but vague images of the more genuine life that is coming.

It has been said that Time has an offspring in her womb we cannot even fancy. That offspring is waiting to be born each day, through each person, within each family, through each community: in us but never from us, through us but never ending in us.

There is a legend told of Leonardo da Vinci that in his great painting of the Last Supper he put such detail into two cups standing on the table that a friend, seeing them, stared at them in open-mouthed amazement. Thereupon, da Vinci seized a brush and with one sweep of his hand painted them out of the picture, crying, "Not that! That isn't what I want you to see! It's the face. Look at the face! Look at Jesus!"[3]

If you recall that painting, you can remember the way all lines move from the outside inward and converge on the face of Christ. Every line directs us to him. No detail of cup or window or disciple is allowed to distract from that center. Yet every line also leads away from that center to the outside. From the Christ to every one of us.

Just as the Lord Christ is set apart from the world and also sent to the world, even so as people of faith, as people of Yahweh God, we are to become genuinely human, that all people might come to know themselves as genuinely human. In the last words of the book of Revelation, the Lord God says to us: I am coming soon.

And so we say, Amen. Come, Lord Jesus. Come!

Notes

1. From Maurice S. Friedman, *Martin Buber: The Life of Dialogue* (New York: Harper Torchbooks/The Cloister Library, [1955] 1960), p. 37.
2. Ibid., p. 95.
3. Paul Scherer, *For We Have This Treasure* (New York: Harper & Row, 1944), p. 137.

CHAPTER FIVE

God's Dream for a Technicolor Society

—Young-IL Kim

Born, reared, and educated in Korea, Young-IL Kim spent six years as a church pastor before coming to the United States at the age of thirty for further study in 1972. He studied for several years each in Oklahoma and New Jersey, and pastored churches in rural Pennsylvania and upstate New York for nine years before coming to the Chicago area in 1984 to serve as director of the Center for Asian-American Ministries at Garrett-Evangelical Theological Seminary. He has been an assistant professor of Church and Society since 1989.

Dr. Kim has experienced cross-cultural differences on several scales. The move from Korea to America presented him with substantial culture shock, because of the vast differences between Korean and American culture, life-style, language, and thought. However, he also experienced cultural differences within the United States. Moving from Oklahoma to New Jersey presented him with a new accent, different landscape, and subtle but distinct differences in culture. Likewise the move from rural Pennsylvania to urban-suburban Chicago provided a striking contrast in cultures. Pastoring a rural church entailed active participation in the lives of the local people, and close interaction. Rural people seemed most helpful, quick to take care of one another. There was a strong sense of community. Life in Chicago is distinctly different, with a much greater sense of the isolation of the individual. The facial expression on the street is typically deadpan. There are also cultural differences between the life of a minister serving a local church and that

70

of a seminary staff and faculty member who is one of many people in similar roles. As the sole minister, Dr. Kim had a sense of being very special in the lives of the church members. In contrast, working on the faculty of a larger institution, he recognized that he is but one of many, without the special recognition and differentiation that go with pastoring a church. All these experiences have given Dr. Kim an understanding and appreciation of the issues in cross-cultural ministry and of the need for all church people to build cross-cultural skills.

Dr. Kim senses that, although the overt ideological expressions of racism in the United States have decreased somewhat over the last few decades, latent or covert racism is still pervasive in American society. He sees this subtle racism in his experiences with Anglo-Saxons who are more than willing to kindly and generously help ethnics when they are in a position of need, but who, when competing on an equal basis, can be quite intolerant. Their attitude seems to be, "We may be equal but we're better." Thanks are due the African Americans who have struggled long and hard to loosen the grip of racism in America and have paved the way for other ethnic groups to participate more fully in this society. Because of their efforts, overt racism has been curtailed, although there has been less progress in dismantling institutionalized structures of racism. In one form or another racism is still alive, and the problems must be acknowledged and addressed.

The following article, "God's Dream for a Technicolor Society," is concerned with pluralism—not religious pluralism, but ethnic and social pluralism. The metaphor of the "melting pot" as an expression of the national American identity, with its emphasis on conformity to Anglo-Saxon culture, has long been popular. However, since the first settlers came to America, consecutive waves of immigrants have merged into American society, all of which have made America not one melting pot, but multiple pots. Thus the real picture of America is a plurality of ethnics and cultures, which may be called a "technicolor society."

Norht American society is the product of immigrants from various countries in the world. The United States is a nation of immigration. Because of the very nature of the United States itself, immigration was destined to play a vital role in its growth. Almost the whole of North American history has been woven by consecutive waves of immigrants, who have come from many different places, times, and ethnic backgrounds.

As immigrants moved onto this North American continent, they brought their inherited customs, languages, religions, and cultures. Accordingly, the culture of the United States became a blend of the myriad cultures of the world, adding one after another, a little at a time. Thus, two factors are clear: North American culture cannot be seen as a monoculture, and it is impossible to study this culture, society, or history without an adequate understanding of immigration.

A Brief History of American Immigration

Since English settlers established Jamestown in 1607, several waves of immigration have taken place, dramatically affecting North American life and society. The first wave (1607–1820), or the Colonial Immigration, consisting of more than forty million persons, came from northwestern European countries. The vast majority of those immigrants were Protestants. They, especially the Pilgrims and Puritans, brought with them their cherished traditions and customs. Their religious, cultural, and social traditions and heritage were firmly implanted in this soil and became the core ethos of North American values and society.[1]

During the same period of time, the slave trade was introducing Africans onto this continent. The first shipload of African slaves to reach America arrived in Jamestown in 1619.

Large-scale forced emigration of Africans to North America began around 1675. Maldwyn Jones says that during the eighteenth century, countless numbers of Africans arrived from the Guinea coast and the West Indies, perhaps as many as 200,000.

The second wave consisted of immigrants who entered the United States between 1820 and 1880. Some historians have named this period the Old Immigration. Strongly correlated with this period were "push-pull" factors. The factors pushing emigrants out of Europe were the poor economic conditions, industrial depressions, poverty, extraordinary increase in population, religious intolerance, demeaning social gradations, and political upheavals. Meanwhile, abundance and opportunity in the United States were pulling the more than thirty-seven million immigrants from European countries.

The third wave, the New Immigration (1880–1930), included about twenty-six million persons entering the United States. Until around 1880, immigrants had originated mostly from northwestern Europe. As the twentieth century approached, however, the ethnicity of the immigrants underwent a marked change, with people arriving mainly from eastern and southern Europe. Unlike the earlier arrivals, most of these new settlers were concentrated in urban areas. The rapid growth of industries in the newly arising North American cities required overseas recruitment. By 1890, for example, one out of three employees in manufacturing and mechanical industries was a third-wave immigrant. This ratio continued until the end of this period.

The fourth wave of immigration, the Recent Immigrants (1930–1990s), has come mostly from Latin American and Asian countries.[2] The year 1965 was pivotal in the history of immigration, especially in immigration from Third World countries. This year marked the beginning of the greatest change in the immigration trends and records of the United States. Namely, the Immigration and Naturalization Act of

1965 abolished discriminatory quotas based on racial and national origin; accordingly, a large number of Asian persons have since come to America.[3] The decade of the 1980s holds the record for the highest number of immigrants. That decade added twelve million more persons from other lands to the population of the United States.[4]

Oftentimes in world history, the socioeconomic-political situation has determined migration trends. Because of the oppression and poverty that existed in the early 1800s in Ireland, more than four million Irish emigrants came to the United States between 1820 and 1920. German immigration began to surge in the middle of the nineteenth century. As were the immigrants before them, most of these Germans were farmers and artisans, but during this time Germany as well as the rest of Europe was undergoing political turmoil. The year 1848 brought along with it the historic revolutions. As the Old Regime regained power, many revolutionists fled their countries. It was for this reason that a significant part of the German immigration at this time comprised political refugees. By 1910, eight million United States citizens were German immigrants or the children of German immigrants.[5]

World War II created some thirty million refugees from Poland, the Baltic states, Belgium, Hungary, and the Netherlands who fled to the United States. Millions of these involuntary immigrants never returned home. Many Chinese also fled from the Communist regime in China in 1948, and many never went back. In 1959, a mass of Cubans fled the Castro takeover, adding to the immigrant population in America. When the South Vietnamese government collapsed at the end of the Vietnam War in 1975 and Vietnamese refugees were evacuated, some thirteen thousand Vietnamese people were gradually placed and settled in America.

All of these immigrants, throughout the centuries, have brought with them their ideas, cultures, and religions, which have shaped North American society.

Two Theories of Assimilation

The Melting Pot theory assumes that there should be one way to be and live in this society, a society in which all individuals and ethnic groups are melded into a new breed, the "American people." This theory has been a hot issue for a long time in the United States. The term "Melting Pot" was coined by Israel Zangwill, an English Jew, who wrote a play called *The Melting Pot*, which had a long run in New York City in 1908.[6] Zangwill's intent was that old-world nationalities of the newly arrived immigrants should be forgotten, since they now lived in the United States, and that all ethnic individuals and groups should be fused into a new superior American nationality.[7] Gunnar Myrdal later affirmed the melting pot theory, and many more people considered the idea of the melting pot to be the destined super-product of United States immigration.[8] Thus, this idea has been a dominant assimilation theory for four or five decades.

The melting pot theory, however, has come under attack since the 1950s by a growing number of sociologists. Ruby Jo Reeves Kennedy, who carried out research on intermarriage trends occurring between 1870 and 1940 in New Haven, Connecticut, reported interesting findings. She argued that while the rate of choosing a mate from the same national origin was decreasing, there was a strong tendency to marry within one's religious group, or, more specifically, one of three principal religious groups: the Protestant, Roman Catholic, and Jewish. She therefore suggested that there was a Triple Melting Pot in this society based on religion.[9]

The triple pot theory was later reinforced by theologian Will Herberg in his book *Protestant-Catholic-Jew* (1955). Herberg suggested that there were three melting pots rather than one in this society, indicating that anyone living in the United States was not really an American if he or she did not belong to one of the three religious groups: Protestant, Catholic, or Jew.

The melting pot theory was even more severely challenged by some philosophers and sociologists in the 1960s. For example, based on the results of their research on ethnic groups in New York City, Nathan Glazer and Daniel P. Moynihan argued that the melting pot phenomenon did not really happen in American society. Rather, the ethnic groups have retained much of their distinct cultural heritage, keeping their ethnic identity. As a result, even though they and their children may lose their native language and some customs, they tend to maintain their family ties, religion, and political interests.[10] The ethnic groups may be assimilated to a large extent, yet the majority of them desire to retain their own religious and cultural traditions as they live in the United States.

Pluralism in the United States

Modern sociological research indicates that United States society has never been a single melting pot, but that many ethnics who immigrate to the United States retain their ethnicity, traditions, cultural practices. For example, the Chinese have built a Chinatown in most of the large cities. Likewise, recent Korean immigrants are building Korea-towns. In Los Angeles they are settling around the Olympic Boulevard. In Chicago, Koreatown centers around Lawrence Street and is rapidly expanding to the northern suburb of Skokie. These immigrants are retaining their ethnicity and enhancing the pluralistic mix of this society. Pluralism is diversity: diversity of peoples and the gifts they bring and share. We need to understand and to appreciate the variety of gifts and their contents. We also need to cherish what gifts we have and to honor what others have.

The Chinese yin-yang philosophy in the book of *Tao-Te*

Ching is an intriguing subject, about the concepts of change and interpersonal relationships as the essence of the cosmic process. Yin is the negative norm, yang is the positive norm; yin is darkness, yang is light; one is passive and the other is active; one is symbolic of earth and the other of heaven; yin is responsiveness, and yang is creativity. The concept of yin-yang can be described in terms of interpersonal relationships. Yin alone cannot be yin; it becomes yin only in relation to yang. Thus, yin and yang are interdependent and inclusive. They are reciprocal. They are harmonious reality. They are *one* in essence but *two* in existence.

Now, this principle of inclusiveness, mutuality, and interpersonal relationship in yin-yang philosophy can be applied to United States society, in which multiethnic groups coexist. We are one in essence, even though there are many different ethnic peoples.

North Americans need to understand the cultural autonomy of the individual ethnic groups. It isn't homogeneity that is wanted, but harmony, in which each individual ethnic group has color, tastes, and rights, which could usher in a truly colorful society. It seems to me that ethnic identity has become more important to Americans in recent years. The fact that many ethnic groups have maintained their identity continuously, instead of letting it disappear within a few generations, demonstrates this trend. Some ethnic groups include a large number of people, so they have no need to adopt the dominant cultural patterns. Thus in North American society, subethnic groups coexist without completely blending; they are "Multi-Color Pots."

Life Meant to Be Ultimately Fair

I am intrigued with the twentieth chapter of Matthew's Gospel. It has become one of my most important resources in devising my Immigrant Theology (see Matt. 20:1-15). The setting is as follows: The owner of a vineyard wanted to hire some workers, so he went out to the marketplace early in the morning. He agreed to pay workers the regular wage, one silver coin a day, and he sent them to work in the vineyard. He went out again at nine o'clock in the morning and saw some people standing there looking for jobs. He told them that if they would work at his farm, he would pay them a fair wage. So they agreed. Then, at twelve o'clock noon and again at three o'clock in the afternoon, the owner did the same thing. Much later, about five o'clock in the afternoon, the owner found some other people out at the marketplace who still could not find work. He brought the workers to the vineyard with the offer of a fair wage.

Then it was time for the owner of the farm to call the workers to receive their wages. The crucial point is this: The workers who had begun to work at five o'clock in the evening were paid a silver coin each, the same amount paid those who were hired early in the morning. Accordingly, the first-comers grumbled, complained, and protested. They claimed that this was unfair treatment. Perhaps they were jealous for they thought that life was unfair, or maybe they did not recognize that life was meant to be ultimately fair before God.

Allow me to allegorize this well-known parable. The vineyard could be seen as the land of America. The owner of the vineyard would be God, the Creator. It seems appropriate to compare the workers of this parable to the immigrants who came to America during different time periods. The workers hired first could be related to the Puritans and Colonists who reached North America before 1820. The nine o'clock workers could be seen as the forced African immigrants. The twelve o'clock workers could be compared to the "Old Immigrants" who came to the United States between 1820 and 1880. The people hired at three o'clock could be related to the "New Immigrants" who arrived between 1880 and 1930 when about twenty-six million persons from Southeast European countries immigrated to North America. Finally, the five o'clock workers could be compared to Hispanics and Asian immigrants. In fact, during the last three decades alone, more than eight million immigrants and refugees have arrived from Asian and South American countries.

As you see, whether we want to recognize it or not, we are all either first-generation immigrants, second-generation immigrants, or the descendants of earlier immigrants. Most anthropologists believe that the first Native Americans also migrated from Asia more than 20,000 years ago. That means we have all come from somewhere, and most of us can trace our roots back to another country. In other words, the population of America today consists entirely of immigrants or the children of the immigrants. As we have seen, the United States is the product of immigration. Its history and society have been woven from successive waves of immigrants.

To construct an immigrant theology, I propose the following five simple premises. The first premise is about *ownership*: Who is the owner of the land of America? The whole earth belongs to God, the Creator; the world is God's farmland. (See Genesis 1; Ps. 8:2-5.) That is to say, the true owner of the vineyard of North America is ultimately God.

The second premise is that the land is a part of *God's creation* and is the gift of God to human beings. Thus, the earth and her fruits are to be shared. It is a basic right of the children of God to have access to the land. For any human being, the first home is the mother's womb. Thereafter, his or her home is the land where he or she stands. I remember a song that goes like this: "This land is my land. This land is your land. . . . This land was made for you and me." The land of North America belongs not only to the people who came at six o'clock and to the nine o'clock workers, but to all her residents.

The third premise is that all North Americans are either

79

immigrants themselves or the descendants of immigrants. There is no exception. In immigrant theology, we must recognize that all persons everywhere are immigrants. When we look at the biblical persons through immigrant eyes, the most important people were immigrants: Abraham, Isaac, Jacob, Joseph, Moses, Ruth, Esther, Ezekiel, Daniel, and many more. Because the Lord told Abraham to "go from your country and your kindred and your father's house," he moved from place to place: from Haran to the land of Canaan, to Egypt, to Canaan, to Hebron, and so on (Genesis 12ff.). Like Abraham's story, there are numerous immigrant stories in the book of Genesis. One remarkable event in Genesis is the immigration of Jacob's children and their families to Egypt by the invitation of Joseph. The book of Ruth is about Ruth, a Moabite woman, who immigrated to Bethlehem and lived there with her mother-in-law. What about the book of Daniel? The main character in the book of Daniel was the young man forced to immigrate to Babylonia who encouraged his people with the hope that God would restore sovereignty to God's people. I could name numerous other stories of immigration in the Bible.

The next premise is that we *experience contempt,* inhospitality, racism, and discrimination, not by the owner, but by the coworkers who were hired a few hours earlier. The important matter is not who arrived there first, or who settled there first. We are equally sons and daughters of God, who is the owner of the land. That means, as members of the same community, we need to share with, to accept, and to understand one another. No one should be pushed out as a marginal person.[11]

The marginalization may occur in very subtle ways. Sometimes I meet people who ask me something like "Where do you come from?" assuming that I am a stranger in this land. I simply reply, "I come from Chicago. Where do *you* come from?" A young graduate student, a second-generation

Korean immigrant, shared this story with me. She was placing an order in a restaurant. After a short conversation, the white waitress said, "Oh! You speak English very well!" "So do you!" the young woman answered.

The last and final premise is about *God's dream.* The owner of the land loves and cares for everyone. The owner wants to pay everyone equally. The owner not only wants to treat everybody evenly, but also craves that everyone be happy, having the same opportunity and freedom. Why did the earlier workers not rejoice that the people who had waited so long in the marketplace now had peace, receiving money to take home to their families? Why did the firstcomers not rejoice that the late arrivals were able to join them?

Some workers might exclaim that life is not fair, because the owner distributed wages equally to each worker. However, he did not pay less than what he had promised to those workers. Rather, he simply offered a premium to some. And more important, every one received the owner's loving-kindness. This is God's *grace,* which is a free gift, undeserved favor, given by God's own will.

The Technicolor Society

When television made its big debut earlier this century, the nature of society reflected the black-and-white screen. Society was separated into black and white. But in the sixties, just when color television was becoming popular, society was becoming more colorful as well. The civil rights movement, the 1965 Immigration Act, which opened the doors to Third World persons, and other events set in motion the formation of a technicolor society.

Color television operates on the basis of three separate colors: red, green, and blue. The different colors are transmitted separately and reassembled on the screen to make a complete picture. The colors remain separate in the

81

picture, but projected on the screen in proximity they appear to the eye as a colorful kaleidoscope of images (*kalos* = beautiful and *eidos* = form).

Much like the technicolor revolution in television and movies, society is undergoing a technicolor revolution. The old idea of the melting pot where everyone goes in different but comes out the same is being discarded. There is a new recognition that while each ethnic group maintains its own identity, traditional culture, and heritage, in the convergence of these multicolor groups the colorful landscape of Americana emerges. Individuals are not transformed into "Americans," but each ethnic group stands distinguishably beside the others, each maintaining its valuable tradition and culture and contributing to North American society.

I live in the northern suburbs of Chicago. We are Korean immigrants. Next door to us lives a family of African American heritage. Next to them is a Jewish family. Across the street is a family of Canadian immigrants. Next to them is a French immigrant family. Their next-door neighbors are of Polish descent. And on our other side is a family from the Philippines. Each family in this miniature sample of our technicolor society maintains its ethnicity, yet we all cooperate together in community events.

Technicolor is a creation of God, of God's design. It is a gift of God to human societies, especially to North American society. God is the one who called the blacks, the yellows, the tans, the whites, and all. The owner of the vineyard gives the workers—the earlier comers and the later comers—the opportunity to accept, to share, and to love one another.

Notes

1. See Max Weber's *The Protestant Ethic and the Spirit of Capitalism*, Talcott Parsons, trans. (New York: Scribner's, 1958). Weber argued that the life-style and value system of the Puritans, which derived from the ideas of Calvinism, had helped capitalism to emerge by giving religious value to hard work, the

discipline of investment, self-denial, and commitment to a profession. Weber stressed there was a certain compatibility between the teachings of Protestantism and the early growth of capitalism in America.

2. This term is mine; no one has named this period of immigration.

3. Discrimination has existed in America almost as long as immigration itself. Of course, the first colonial pioneers had no difficulty with this problem, but as soon as permanent settlements sprang up in the wilderness of the New World, strangers were treated if not with hostility, often with a guarded caution. In this land where the Caucasians became the hosts, the Oriental Mongoloids faced the toughest discriminatory treatments. It was particularly the physical and extreme cultural differences that made the Oriental immigrants conspicuous wherever they went. The Asian people have been hounded by discriminatory attitudes until they were barred completely from immigrating to America. In 1882, for example, the Chinese Exclusion Act was passed by the United States. This was the first time in America that a whole nationality was kept from landing on its shores. This act was renewed in 1892 and again in 1902 for an indefinite period of time. In 1924 the Johnson-Reed Act prohibited, among other things, the immigration of any persons ineligible for citizenship, which included all the Asians. Discriminatory legislation did not end here. Perhaps the most discriminating and flagrant violation of human rights occurred with the signing of the executive order 9066. All people of Japanese descent in 1942 were forced out of their homes and required to spend two years in internment camps.

4. Ronald Takaki, *Strangers from a Different Shore: A History of Asian Americans* (New York: Penguin Books, 1989), pp. 420-71.

5. John F. Kennedy, *A Nation of Immigrants* (New York: Popular Library, 1964), p. 16.

6. Israel Zangwill, *The Melting Pot* (New York: Macmillan, 1925).

7. The word *ethnic*, which means a nation or race, can be traced to the Greek term *ethnikos*.

8. Gunnar Myrdal, *An American Dilemma* (1944; reprint, New York: McGraw-Hill, 1964).

9. Ruby Jo Reeves Kennedy, "Single or Triple Melting Pot? Intermarriage Trends in New Haven, 1870–1940," *American Journal of Sociology* 49 no. 4 (January 1944): 331-39.

10. Nathan Glazer and Daniel Patrick Moynihan, *Beyond the Melting Pot: The Negros, Puerto Ricans, Jews, Italians, and Irish of New York City* (Cambridge, Mass.: M.I.T. and Harvard University Press, 1963).

11. The philosophical concept of "marginal situations" *(Grenzsituationen)* is derived from Karl Jaspers (see esp. his *Philosophie*, 1932). Martin Heidegger discussed the concept of death as the most important marginal situation (see his *Sein und Zeit*, 1929). The sociological concept of "marginal man" was first devised by Robert E. Park in "Human Migration and the Marginal Man," *American Journal of Sociology* 33 no. 6 (May 1928): 881-93. It was later elaborated by Everett V. Stonequist in *The Marginal Man* (New York: Charles Scribner's Sons, 1937). The concept of the marginal person is the one who remains at the edges or margins of two cultural worlds and who is full member of neither. Accordingly, the marginal persons are not fully accepted by the dominant society.

CHAPTER SIX

A Narrative Approach to Pastoral Care in an Intercultural Setting

—Edward P. Wimberly

Edward P. Wimberly draws on sixteen years of experience in teaching at theological institutions to address the needs of the ethnically different student. He is concerned that some of the presuppositions about traditional theological education need to be addressed. For example, he makes a distinction between intercultural education and experiential education. Experiential education, prevalent in today's approach to theological education, assumes a similarity of ethnic and cultural background of its participants. In the experiential model, the experiences of the ethnically and culturally different are ignored when they differ from the majority's common experience. However, intercultural education assumes that the cultural background of the participants in theological education is very important. An intercultural educational approach assumes that the experiences of the culturally different must be addressed and not ignored. Therefore, Dr. Wimberly presents a narrative model of intercultural education to ensure that ethnically diverse educational experiences are considered.

This article addresses this problem, which many students from different ethnic backgrounds face in theological education. An intercultural approach rooted in the student's own experience and using the narrative approach is presented as a way to be more sensitive to the needs of the culturally different student. The key point of this article is that seminary faculty and ethnically different students need to be aware of the fact that they are teaching and learning two different languages in theological education.

Dr. Wimberly earned a B.A. from the University of Arizona and an S.T.B., S.T.M., and Ph.D. from Boston University. His cross-cultural experiences include serving as exchange minister to West Germany. Formerly Associate Professor of Pastoral Care at Garrett-Evangelical Theological Seminary and Director of the Center for the Church and the Black Experience, Dr. Wimberly is currently Professor of Pastoral Care and Counseling at the Interdenominational Theological Center in Atlanta, Georgia.

W hen I entered seminary in the mid 1960s, I encountered my first black professor since grammar school. I had gone through high school and college without encountering a black professor. Entering Boston University School of Theology, I was fortunate to meet this professor, who said something that has remained with me over the years. He said that seminary education was like learning a second language. What he meant was that seminary education had a language of its own, one that was different from the normal everyday language that I used.

The statement of this black professor freed me to pursue theological education recognizing that I did not have to discount my own way of learning or the culture out of which I had come. What I now understood was that there was a way of approaching academic pursuits that involved learning in a way that was different from that to which I had been accustomed. I was to pursue theological education learning a new language, but I was also given permission to bring the experiences that I had as a black person into the academic curriculum to analyze these experiences by employing that new language.

For many years I was satisfied to use categories provided by my discipline to analyze black experiences. The discipline served me well. I also tried to give these categories cultural respectability by drawing comparisons to similar processes in the black experience. But, at speaking engagements around the country, I encountered a great deal of criticism of this approach from black students. They were saying that I was applying categories from the dominant culture that did not do justice to the experiences of black people in the United States, who had a cultural heritage from Africa. I listened to this critique with interest and agreement. However, I had no idea how to employ categories that were indigenous to black culture that did not also have some influence from the wider culture. Therefore, I proceeded to write and lecture employing the categories of my discipline, thinking that devising an indigenous language specific to black people was not possible.

There does appear to be, however, a way to draw on the black indigenous approach to language as part of the academic process. A narrative approach seems to offer a way of including divergent cultural backgrounds without having to subject human experience to categories of the discipline prematurely. There is no way to avoid using the categories of the discipline at some point in theological education. However, there is an opportunity to help students organize their experiences into categories that are specific to their culture prior to subjecting them to so-called alien categories.

The narrative approach has enabled me to pay particular attention to how I as a black person have learned and how I have appropriated my indigenous language and categories in the academic process. From a methodological viewpoint it is not only possible to use academic categories to analyze my own experience and the experiences of black people; it is also possible to draw into the academic work the natural ways in which black people learn and communicate.

I have begun this presentation autobiographically because it helps to highlight the chief presupposition undergirding my approach to teaching and learning in theological education from an intercultural perspective. The chief presupposition is that most black students, ethnic minority students, and international students of color generally have

86

had the same experiences I confronted when I began theological studies. That is to say, these students enter a world where they have to learn a new language and a new way of looking at the world that is different from the way they look at the world within their own ethnic communities. Therefore, I have felt it my task as a teacher of multicultural students to introduce the ethnic minority students and international students of color to this new seminary world as clearly as possible, recognizing that these students are learning a second language.

I don't assume that any student either from the dominant culture or from ethnic minority cultures has been exposed to this new academic language and world view. In order to present the course as a second language, I introduce some of the leading presuppositions of the course as well as the new vocabulary that is the basis of this new language.

Introducing course material as a second language is not enough for black and other ethnic minority students of color, however. There is need to find a way to give ethnic minority students and international people of color permission to draw their own personal ways of learning and experiencing reality into the academic process. The task is not to be sequential, such that the new language and world view are presented first. Rather, the task is to help the student to appropriate her or his personal learning and experiences in the learning process at the same time as the new language and vocabulary are being introduced. The point is that it is important to facilitate learning that is simultaneous and not sequential. Applied theological learning is often sequential and linear. However, learning from an intercultural perspective needs to be mutual, relating theory and experience at the same time.

I have also discovered that many majority-culture students, both male and female, seem to appreciate an approach to classroom teaching that introduces material as if it were a second language rather than the native language of the student. Moreover, the students also appreciate the permission to appropriate their own way of learning and experiencing in the learning endeavor. Perhaps the reasons many theological students respond to this approach as a general rule are that they are older, many are female, and many are second-career people who have been away from the academic world a number of years. I have found that many women, ethnic students, and second-career people like learning that integrates experience and concepts.

Introducing a course as a second language and giving students permission to draw their own way of learning and experiencing into the process are the principal ways I have approached intercultural theological education. It is student and learner focused. However, one cannot assume that experiential education is the same as intercultural education. Experiential education assumes that the cultural backgrounds of the learners are the same. Intercultural education assumes that the cultural backgrounds of the learners are not the same. Moreover, an intercultural approach to theological education not only encourages the student to bring his or her own experiences into the academic process. It also encourages the student to bring the specific indigenous cultural values at work within the ethnic minority community to bear on the subject matter.[1] Encouraging the student to add her or his distinctive cultural values and world view to the dialogue with the world view of the course material facilitates optimum learning for the ethnic student as well as for others. Such an intercultural approach lends itself to student creativity as well as contributes to making the course material relevant to the circumstances from which the ethnic minority student comes.

Providing an atmosphere where other students can witness this intercultural process at work is essential to increasing the cross-cultural learning of all students. This can be done in a variety of ways. However, the best way is to begin early in the course to invite ethnic minority students as well as others to add the world views of their indigenous cultures to the dialogue with the course content in writing assignments, in small groups, and in class discussion. Moreover, it is important to prepare students from the dominant culture to be open to the intercultural dialogue without feeling that their values are under attack. I have found that open intercultural dialogue, where students feel free to add their indigenous values and world views to the dialogue with the values in the course, frees the student from the dominant culture to explore how her or his values are different from those that are presented in the course. This is very true for those white female students who are attempting to discern what a feminine approach to pastoral care might be.

To summarize, the intercultural approach to teaching pastoral care and counseling in a theological curriculum involves (1) teaching the course as a second language that is different from the student's indigenous language; (2) enabling simultaneous integration of the student's experience with the course content; (3) encouraging intercultural dialogue between the student's indigenous world view and the world view of the course material; and (4) facilitating an open classroom for intercultural dialogue.

I have found that the best way to facilitate the four dimensions of an intercultural approach to teaching pastoral care and counseling is the narrative approach. Such an approach enables the student to bring her or his indigenous way of learning and experiencing into the intercultural process and at the same time prepare the ground for adding the indigenous world view to the dialogue with the world view of the course. Encouraging all the students to share their own stories within the course in small groups also facilitates the cross-cultural learning.

Although the narrative approach to teaching pastoral care

89

and counseling lends itself to intercultural teaching and learning, it is necessary to spell out in further detail the philosophical and theological grounds for a narrative approach. Second, it is important to share what a course embodying an intercultural approach might look like. I have chosen to present a course that I teach in marriage and family counseling to illustrate an intercultural approach to teaching pastoral care and counseling in a theological seminary.

A Narrative Approach

A narrative approach to learning and teaching is basic to understanding the four dimensions of the intercultural approach. A narrative orientation is an oral way to approach learning and teaching that is central to the way in which many black and other ethnic minorities and international students of color learn and experience.[2] Black people and other ethnic minorities and international people of color live in cultural environments that make storytelling and listening to stories the primary vehicle for teaching, learning, and moral development. An oral approach shapes ethnic persons' identity and provides a basis for giving each person an orientation to life. Moreover, an oral approach is relational in that it takes place in a network of caring relationships, and storytelling and listening to stories reinforce the relational bonds that exist within families and extended family networks.

Although an oral and narrative approach characterizes the way ethnic minority people—African Americans, Native Americans, Hispanic Americans, and Asian Americans—approach communication, learning, and experience, an ocular approach seems to be the dominant style that characterizes theological education.[3] Bringing students from an oral culture into an ocular academic learning and teaching environment requires that a special set of skills be given the ethnic minority and international student of color. Fortunately, the ethnic minority and international students have been to college and are, therefore, somewhat familiar with the ocular approach. However, ministry not only requires ocular skills such as analysis and abstracting, but it also requires the ability to relate in oral ways and carry out ministry in cultures to which many ethnic minority and international students of color will return. It must also be pointed out that many local churches, whether of the dominant culture or of ethnic minority cultures, are oral in communications style.[4] Students in general need to build oral and ocular skills within theological education.

Ocular skills include cognitive and perceptive skills.[5] These skills include the ability to think analytically, paying attention to parts and specifics, the ability to abstract and extract shared features from the concrete, and the ability to assign names to these shared features. Ocular skills include ignoring the unique and idiosyncratic in favor of creating categories for shared features. It is interested in describing shared features and emphasizes objectivity. Meaning depends on lasting words, and communication can take place without any attention to relationships or nonverbal content.

In contrast to ocular ways of cognition and perception, oral styles are relational, subjective, and concrete. There is attention to uniqueness, and words and concepts have personal meaning and relevance to the learner. Meaning is related to specific contexts, and making generalizations to other contexts is not as important. Parts have very little meaning apart from specific contexts. The whole picture seems to be more important than the parts. Responses tend to be affective, and there is a participatory way of learning. Drama and the use of the whole body in communication seem to be central to an oral way of thinking and communicating. People with oral styles tend to be more proficient in using expressive forms of self-communication, and visual arts are important to the learner. Performance styles along with the use of metaphors, images, and stories are important dimensions of this orientation. Concern for freedom, novelty, personal distinctiveness, and oral-aural modes of learning and communication also distinguish the oral from the ocular approach to cognition and perception.

It is clear that theological education is proficient in the ocular style of cognition and perception. This cannot be changed, but there needs to be more balance between the ocular and the oral styles of learning and teaching for all theological students regardless of their cultural backgrounds. Moreover, as ethnic minority and international students of color become more proficient in the ocular, analytically oriented style, this proficiency should not come at the expense of the oral, relational style of many of the ethnic minority and international students. Theological education will have to become more skilled in integrating both cognitive and perceptive styles, and the curriculum needs to reflect this integration because of the demands of ministry.

A Narrative Approach to Theologizing

Theological education not only needs to integrate the ocular and the oral in better ways to respond to the needs of ministry. Theological education also needs to pay close attention to the way in which students theologize. This is especially true for ethnic minority students and international students of color.

An oral-relational style of cognition and perception often means that the natural and indigenous style of engaging in theology within the cultural environment is narrative in form. A narrative approach to theology is the hermeneutical use of story or stories as a means of interpreting reality and giving meaning to life within a religious frame of reference.[6] It is an approach to theological thinking where ethnic minority people and international students of color use a central story for interpreting all of life and reality for the purposes of finding meaning in existence. Narrative theology, then, is story interpreting story. It involves how God's participation in history influences the concrete lives of ethnic minority people and international people of color and the ways these people give expression to this encounter with God in history.

The contrast between the methods of narrative theology and the methods of academic theology generally employed in theological education cannot be overemphasized. Academic theology employs an analytical, scientific, and ocular approach to theologizing. Abstract categories are essential, and reflection is often linear. Written documents and reading are highly valued, and theological discourse is usually undertaken through reading highly technical papers that have definitional precision. In contrast, narrative theology is oral. It takes place in the form of storytelling, and it often takes the form of preaching. It is contextual and concrete. It focuses on how people have experienced God in their daily lives. Its content is found in metaphor, image, and story.

The significance of this prolonged ocular analysis is not to play down the role of the analytical and technical; rather, the goal is to highlight the fact that there are two ways of learning and that ethnic minority students and international students of color in the United States may be more at home with one style than with the other. The goal is to include both dimensions—cognition and perception—not only to facilitate intercultural learning, but also for the sake of the local church that may be very oral in its manner of communicating and relating. Both styles are appropriate in theological education. Students as well as professors need to be proficient in both.

Employing both ocular and oral methods in theological education requires a theory of communication that embraces both methods. A rhetorical approach to communication can em-

93

brace both styles and can enable course content to serve both ends.

A Rhetorical Approach to Teaching

Rhetoric refers to the vehicle that is used to communicate messages. Rhetorical communication can be oral as well as written. Key in a rhetorical approach to communication is the listener and the reader, who are the objects of the communication.[7] The vehicle that I use to communicate the content of courses I teach is focused on the student. Not only are my courses student-focused, they also attempt to help the student employ her or his own native cognitive and perceptive styles as an initial way to approach the subject matter.

A student-focused approach to teaching takes seriously the content and the subject matter to be communicated, but it also recognizes that it is through rhetoric that the message is given. Therefore, there are some rhetorical assumptions that undergird my approach to subject matter and the student.

Students bring with them much learning, much knowledge as well as a continuing dialogue with God that helps truth to unfold in their lives. I see subject matter as an evocative trigger for calling students' attention to the truth that is unfolding within them. Subject matter, in this view of rhetoric, is a vehicle to help students pay attention to that truth and growth occurring in their lives.

As a student-focused vehicle, the rhetorical use of subject matter is not coercive. It does not seek to impose on the student concepts and methods that ignore the student's own indigenous ways of understanding reality and communicating. Rather, I ask students to add their own stories and ways of undertaking theology to the dialogue with the subject matter. I then ask them to pick and choose those concepts and theories that are consistent with their life experience and that make sense to them at the moment. If students find that the subject matter violates their own indigenous approach, I then ask them to indicate why the subject matter does not relate to them and then I ask them to find appropriate subject matter from the discipline or other relevant disciplines.

Another important assumption about rhetoric that I hold is that students need stories, images, metaphors, and concepts to interpret their experiences as well as to express these experiences. Introducing concepts and analytical methods into the learning process that respect the indigenous ways students learn and communicate provides them with ways to evaluate their stories and helps them to see areas of needed growth. Analytical methods can help them evaluate their lives, and they can appropriate the subject matter for releasing the growth-facilitating aspects of their indigenous stories and styles of learning. At the same time such an evaluation decreases the impact of growth-inhibiting factors that block learning.

It is crucial that black students, ethnic students, and international students of color appropriate, evaluate, and reappropriate their indigenous styles of cognition, learning, and communicating. There are many reasons for this conclusion that have sound psychological and educational foundations.

The first rationale is that the psychology of consciousness recognizes that the whole brain is involved in learning.[8] For example, a neurolinguistic approach to learning, communication, and cognition focuses on the language of the left brain and the language of the right brain. Left-brain language is characterized by an analytic style.[9] This style emphasizes complete sentences with appropriate grammatical structure—subject, verb, object. The language of the left brain is formal, exact, precise, and orderly. Emphasis is on objective form and conceptual content.

Right-brain language, on the other hand, is characterized by a flowing style rather than by an analytic style.[10] A flowing

95

style is informal, vivid, suggestive, and imaginative. Subjectivity is more of a factor than is objectivity. Drama, story, paradox, and parables are the modes of communication. The immediate moment is important, and relationships between people influence the way one communicates, learns, and perceives. Thinking and formulating ideas are more metaphorical, and images are used to convey ideas.

In right-brain language, memory and recall for non-Western people and ethnic minorities in academic settings tend to improve when folkstory style is used.[11] The reason for this is that, in these cultures, stories provide the structure for organizing memory and recall.

The point of this is to say that culture reinforces the functioning of the brain. Western culture reinforces the analytic brain functions while non-Western and oral cultures tend to support the more fluid brain functions. The key is to recognize that both left and right brain functioning are operative in the learning and perceiving processes.

It is important to know that ethnic minority students and non-Western students often learn better if their oral and fluid styles of cognition and perception are involved in the teaching and learning. This means that both styles must be presented. Emphasis on just the analytic style encourages the student to learn only an abstract language that will not be viewed as relevant or necessary. Fluid and relational learning is more natural and helpful to ethnic minorities and non-Western students. Therefore, both teaching and learning need to draw on both sides of the brain simultaneously to best aid learning and teaching.

A theory of learning and teaching rooted in a narrative approach seems to benefit ethnic minority and non-Western students who have grown up as part of oral cultures. The way many of these students learn and become fully involved in the learning process is through storytelling and listening. The chief area left for exploration from a theoretical perspective is the way in which storytelling and listening to stories are employed in the teaching and learning of pastoral care and counseling.

Autobiography and Biography

Autobiography and biography are the principal methods of approaching pastoral care and counseling from a narrative perspective.[12] In autobiography, a person tells his or her story through oral or written means. In biography, a person tells another person's story through written or oral means. By their very nature biography and autobiography are narrative methods. They report events and are given significance as events are retold in light of the present circumstances that a person faces.

Pastoral care and counseling are autobiographical and biographical in nature. Charles Gerkin has highlighted the fundamental basis of pastoral care and counseling as the case study.[13] Case study is largely a narrative approach using biography and autobiography. Through autobiography the counselee or parishioner tells his or her story orally. Through biographical means, the counselor records the relevant information from the counselee-parishioner and pieces together a holistic picture that is eventually fed back to the counselee-parishioner for that person to refine and modify for the purpose of growth. Parishioner-counselee growth comes as a result of telling stories and putting the stories into some larger perspective that makes sense.

The linking of case study to the narrative approach has been accomplished in the work of James Hillman.[14] His chief contribution is the way in which he links case study to plot. For him the plot is the "why" that gives meaning and purpose to one's existence. According to Hillman, by telling his or her story the person in therapy does not hope to achieve identity or

97

healing; rather, that person is seeking a soul story or a plot. That is, people want to know how their own lives are attached to significance. In Hillman's view, our primary motivation in life is to find the purpose for our existence. If we find the purpose for our existence, then we can find a reason to keep on living.

From a theological perspective the significance of one's life or the plot of one's life is derived from an encounter with God's unfolding plot. Our life takes on meaning and character as we see *our story* in light of *the Story*.

From the perspective of theology, autobiography, biography, and case study, plot or meaning emerges within pastoral counseling and care when the counselee-parishioner visualizes clearly how her or his story is linked to God's unfolding story. The discovery of the relationship of one's autobiography with God's autobiography in the midst of caring and counseling is what makes pastoral counseling and care religious.

Discovery of plot is the key to the case study approach to pastoral care and counseling. It is not enough for the person to tell or write his or her own story. The goal is for the person to find significance and meaning. The role of the pastoral counselor is to help in the significance-finding venture. Therefore, the role of the pastoral caregiver and counselor is to help the counselee-parishioner let his or her story unfold *(unfolding of plot)*; help her or him piece together events as the story unfolds *(linking of plot)*; help her or him account for the potentially alien dimensions that have entered the story *(thickening of plot)*; and help him or her see how God is transforming what has happened to the person into something positive *(twisting of plot)*. The role of the pastoral counselor and caregiver is to help in the unfolding, linking, thickening, and twisting of the plot in a person's life as he or she searches for significance.

The same is true for the professor who teaches pastoral care and counseling from a narrative perspective. The student has

98

a story. She or he is a living case study in search of a meaning or a plot. Therefore, the role of the teacher is to create an environment where the student can discern and discover his or her plot. In theological education, from the perspective of ethnic minority students and international students of color, this means helping them discern the connection between their own unfolding lives and the unfolding of God's life. The course material and classroom environment become the principal means for helping students discover this important connection.

A Course in Marriage and Family Counseling

I teach a course entitled "Pastor as Counselor: Pre-Marriage, Marriage, and Family Counseling." The basic presupposition of the course is that the best way to enable students to learn marriage and family skills and knowledge is to begin with what they have already brought to the classroom. That is, the students were born into families and have learned the skills and knowledge that will help them in learning marriage and family counseling skills and knowledge.

The course begins as an autobiographical course where students reengage their family-of-origin experiences of growing up. From these experiences the student draws out certain meaning that then becomes the basis of reflection for the course. At some point the theory that students learn in the course begins to interact with their family experiences, and they begin to relate theory and experience. In this way the narrative approach and a more analytic approach are related simultaneously.

Non-Western students are encouraged to participate in the autobiographical experience of the family of origin. They are also encouraged to use the concepts from course content in their reflecting if they are relevant. If the concepts are not relevant, they are encouraged to find material more specific to family cultural patterns and values in the indigenous culture.

99

Once this is done, we find ways in small groups to share what the students have learned from this experiential instruction.

There are specific theories and approaches to teaching marriage and family counseling that I think lend themselves to the intercultural approach. These theories and approaches include a systems approach, the family-of-origin paper, family sculpting, and family genogram. The remainder of this essay briefly introduces these ideas.

A Systems Approach

A systems approach to marriage and family dynamics views the family as a whole with structures and functions.[15] Individuals are unique in themselves, but in systems theory individuals are viewed as part of a complete family system. This complete family system is multigenerational and includes the extended family as well as augmented or fictive kinship networks. Structures of interaction, relating, family values, and family myths and values are explored for their impact on family members.

One of the basic assumptions of a systems approach to family dynamics is that well-functioning families are those families that have well-developed communication patterns, firm boundaries separating individuals and generations, and strong self-concepts among the adults, who know who they are apart from one another. Family members are related to other family members in ways that free all to be themselves. Children are valued and respected, and parents who can be parents are aware of the developmental needs of their children. Boundaries between older generations are firm but flexible, permitting relationship across generations. Roles are distinct, but flexible, based on the situation in families.

The course in marriage and family for seminary students seeks to help the student explore her or his own life as a family member from a systems perspective. Differing perspectives among systems family therapists are examined by students. The goal is to find those ideas and concepts that are appropriate to the student's own growth as a family member.

Helping the Student Get in Touch with Family of Origin

The family-of-origin paper is one way to help the student reengage her or his family of origin. It is an academic and experiential exercise that helps the seminary student explore her or his family of birth and relationships with significant family members, crises, and events. It is multigenerational. Those students who were reared by foster parents or by extended family members are encouraged to explore the relationships, events, and crises with extended family members and fictive kin.

The purpose of this exercise is to help the student explore the influence of the family of origin on his or her current choices including selection of mate, current interactional patterns with those outside the family of origin, and the choice of ministry as a profession.

As students are writing the family-of-origin paper, they are encouraged to employ genogram and sculpting methods in small groups to recall family-of-origin material. A family genogram is a structural diagram of a person's generational relationship system. It is autobiographical and oral in character, lending itself very easily to the intercultural narrative styles of ethnic minority students and international students of color. It is multigenerational, tracing significant relational patterns across many generations. Because it is a diagram, one can diagrammatically portray information such as names, ages, marriages, divorces, deaths, important events, and crises. Moreover, family myths, values, and traditions can be explored multigenerationally. The genogram helps ethnic

101

minority students and international students of color bring out significant indigenous cultural values.

Family sculpting is different from the genogram in that it is a dramatic tool designed to portray the arrangement of family members at a particular point in time. The purpose of sculpting is to portray family interaction using objects or people from a small group to help students reexperience their role and position in their current family or family of origin. The student is encouraged to use members of the class to portray and talk about family concerns. It is both an oral and non-oral exercise. Class members put class members in roles and positions that non-verbally represent what the student believes to be real, and then the student talks about what it feels like to arrange or sculpt a family.

Systems theory, the family-of-origin paper, the genogram, and the sculpting are ideas and methods that I use interculturally. Family systems theory has ideas that are compatible with extended family and fictive family relationships characteristic of many ethnic minority students and international students of color. Moreover, the genogram and sculpting help these students gain access to family material in oral and participatory ways. More than this, the family-of-origin paper enables students to combine experiential and analytic skills in the learning process. In short, the paper uses both hemispheres of the brain.

In conclusion, an intercultural approach to pastoral care recognizes the experiences, values, and indigenous culture of ethnic minority students and international students of color. It takes seriously the oral nature of the learning and teaching process. It also respects the divergent learning styles of students. It helps the student build analytic skills, but not at the expense of relational skills. It teaches course material as a second language, and it enables simultaneous integration of the student's experience and course content. It encourages intercultural dialogue in the classroom, and it facilitates the comparison of non-Western world views with Western perspectives within the course.

Notes

1. David Augsburger in *Pastoral Counseling Across Cultures* (Philadelphia: Westminster Press, 1986) makes a distinction between experiencing something within a Western context and experiencing something that is not within the Western context. Experience in a non-Western culture includes different beliefs, values, and world view that one must bring into the academic process. See pp. 29-30.
2. The value of a narrative approach as the language of many ethnic peoples has been highlighted in the following works. Taylor and June McConnell, *Family Ministry Through Cross-Cultural Education* (Evanston, Ill.: Leiffer Bureau of Social and Religious Research, Garrett-Evangelical Theological Seminary, 1986), pp. 32-33; and Anne and Edward Wimberly, *One Household One Hope: Building Ethnic Minority Clergy Family Support Networks* (Nashville: Division of Ordained Ministry, The United Methodist Church, 1988).
3. For a description of the ocular approach, see Clarence Rivers, "The Oral African Tradition Versus the Ocular Tradition," in *This Far by Faith: American Black Worship and Its African Roots* (Washington, D.C.: National Office for Black Catholics, 1977), pp. 38-49.
4. Jim Hopewell, *Congregations: Stories and Structures* (Philadelphia: Fortress Press, 1987), pp. 3-18.
5. For a description of ocular skills, see Janice Hale, *Black Children* (Salt Lake City: Brigham Young University Press, 1982), pp. 30-44.
6. For an introduction to narrative theology, see Michael Goldberg, *Theology and Narrative: A Critical Introduction* (Nashville: Abingdon, 1981).
7. The theory of rhetoric comes from Augustine's theory of rhetoric. See James J. Murphy, *Rhetoric in the Middle Ages* (Berkeley: University of California Press, 1974), pp. 286-91.
8. James B. Ashbrook, *The Human Mind and the Mind of God* (Lanham, Md.: University Press of America, 1984), pp. 41-60.
9. Ibid., p. 55.
10. Ibid.
11. Robert L. Munroe and Ruth H. Munroe, *Cross-Cultural Human Development* (New York: Jason Aronson, 1977), p. 87.
12. Goldberg in *Theology and Narrative* explores in depth the role of autobiography in narrative. See pp. 62-145.
13. Charles V. Gerkin, *The Living Human Document* (Nashville: Abingdon Press, 1984), pp. 25-35.
14. James Hillman, *Healing Fiction* (Barrytown, N.Y.: Station Hill Press, 1983), pp. 9-12.
15. See Edward P. Wimberly, *Pastoral Counseling and Spiritual Values* (Nashville: Abingdon, 1982), pp. 104-55.

CHAPTER SEVEN

The African Principle of Existence-in-Relation as a Model for Cross-Cultural Ministry

—Nolbert Kunonga

Nolbert Kunonga is an Anglican priest from Zimbabwe who is currently working on a graduate degree at Garrett-Evangelical Theological Seminary. He trained as a priest at United Theological Seminary in Zimbabwe, graduating in 1978. The Reverend Mr. Kunonga also holds a Certificate in Social Work, conferred jointly by the Harare School of Social Work and the University of Zimbabwe, where he graduated in 1979. Continuing his studies at that university, he acquired a B.S. in sociology in 1983, and a B.A. with honors in Religious Studies in 1989.

The Reverend Mr. Kunonga has worked for the Anglican Church of Zimbabwe in various capacities. Prior to becoming a priest, he was a catechist or evangelist at Avondale Parish Church in Harare. After ordination he served as associate rector at St. Monica Parish, Seke. In 1983–84, while studying in the Boston area, he worked as an associate rector of Ascension Memorial Church in Ipswich, Massachusetts.

Returning to Zimbabwe in 1984, he worked for the diocese, and then served as rector of St. Martin's Parish Church from 1985 to 1990. During that time he was elected a member of the Diocesan Standing Committee and also of the Bishop's Senate, worked as the bishop's examining chaplain, and in 1989 was appointed the bishop's archdeacon of Harare Diocese West, with responsibility for twenty parishes. He also served as a part-time teacher at Goal House Seminary and the University Evening School.

In this article, the Reverend Mr. Kunonga devises a model

of cross-cultural ministry based on the African concept of existence-in-relation. As the God *Mwari* exists in relation to the human community, so do human beings find meaning, identity, and purpose in relationship with other persons. All humans have their origin in *Guruuswa*, the center of all existence, and find a sense of social solidarity and empathy with one another's suffering and pain through the stomach and the internal organs.

Hence, cross-cultural ministry takes the form of the wounded healer, sharing the experience both of being victimized by the racist images of white dominance and black inferiority communicated by the colonial culture and of struggling with Christ to reverse and reorder the injustice and inequity of a mentality and social order imposed by the colonial powers.

This creative synthesis of traditional African religious concepts, current process theology, and a pastoral psychology centered in empathy, provides an approach to cross-cultural ministry that is distinctively African and also provides helpful guidance to pastoral ministry in any local congregation.

The following story is told by a Kikuyu friend from Kenya. It is linked with the Kikuyu rite of passage in which he participated at the birth of his son.

My wife Sarah started labor pains and my little sister was sent to summon a nearby midwife. My mother and the midwife prepared water for cleansing. My wife was washed, and my firstborn son was born. My mother asked me as father to cut five pieces of sugar cane. My wife took the sugar cane juice into her mouth, and with it fed our newborn baby. Then the placenta was removed and buried in uncultivated land near our hut.

The midwife took the child, bathed, and oiled him. I took a goat, and in the presence of the whole family and some members of our village, I sacrificed it to thank the ancestors and

God. My father, who was the oldest member of our clan, took some of the meat and some water and placed them on the ground for the ancestors to join us in the meal. He told the spirits that the child was born to the community, to the spirits, and to God, and that the child was theirs as much as he was mine.

The medicine woman was called to purify our hut. The cleaning of the hut, the bathing of my wife and our son, the washing of her clothes, and the moving of our fire from place to place were stopped. My wife and son were secluded in the hut for at least five days. At the end of the seclusion, my wife's head was shaved and she took her first post-natal bath. All was cleansed, and my wife and our son were welcomed back into the community.[1]

This experience is indicative of the African principle of existence-in-relation, for it points to the vital relationship which the African maintains with nature, *Mwari*-God, the deities, the ancestors, the tribe, the clan, the extended family, and the nuclear family.[2]

In the world view reflected in this birth rite, the African enters each of these entities with his or her whole being without recognizing the existence of any boundaries dividing one from the other. Here every woman or man is a piece of a whole system, a system in which people know that they are a resource to one another and are bound together with nature, ancestors, and deity in a vital and life-giving synergy. The child is born to the whole community. The sacrifice denotes a thanksgiving to ancestors and to God, and also an incorporation into the human community. Both the living dead—the ancestors—and God participate and are acknowledged in the pouring of the libation.

To describe this African view of existence-in-relation is no simple task, for the notion encompasses within it a great deal, practically the whole universe. The implication of this remarkable thesis is that in the African world view, the primary source for coping and dealing with pain, suffering, and wounds is in one another. For the African, one's personal, as well as sacramental, presence is the most important thing one can offer to another.

The idea of sacrament here is crucial in this model; it presupposes wounds and grace. This is an African way of expressing David Augsburger's model for cross-cultural ministry of the wounded healer.[3] The African notion of existence-in-relation, or the principle of the human person-in-relation, is the African community's way of talking about Augsburger's concept of my woundedness and my healer in relation to your woundedness and your healer. As Augsburger puts it, "My woundedness will not infect yours but will stand with you in presence and understanding; my healer . . . will call out the healing forces within you."[4] As we come to or cross over to the other, we bring him or her both wounds and grace, and he or she in turn brings us wounds and grace.

To propose the African world view as a basis for cross-cultural ministry is to confirm Augsburger's contention that "all cultures are within God's care." No race, no culture, and no world view is outside the presence of God, and "every culture offers background to the saving work of God."[5]

Here we are affirming a ministry that is universal in quality. Yet at the same time, being African, it is also local. Such a ministry is also personal, in the sense that either a person or a group can come to another in a sacramental form, whereby the wounded-healer paradox is offered reciprocally; that is, the minister is healed as he or she heals.

A Wounded Healer in a Colonial Culture

What is fundamental at this point is that we have a theology that relates at one and the same time to all situations, to all humankind, to a local culture, and to a particular person. This concept undermines what may be termed "colonial culture," which projects a view that other religions, such as African traditional religions, are false and have nothing to offer. Such an assumption is dangerous, because its beginning point is negative and it makes Jesus the enemy of other cultures. In the framework of the African world view, we proclaim a Christ who speaks the local African language, as well as both the universal language of all humankind and the intimately personal language of the individual. I worship a Christ who includes, challenges, clarifies, completes, and consummates the healing, liberation, and transformation of all of humankind.

As an African, I see myself as already a wounded healer, by virtue of the fact that, like the people to whom I minister, I am a victim of and bear the scars of colonial culture. The discussion of Donald Messer on being wounded healers suggests that it is the victim of colonial culture who understands the language of the other victims of colonial culture.[6] But one can move beyond being a victim, because, by the African logic of existence-in-relation, one has also received the healing power from others and this becomes one's healing. An African who is looked to as a leader not only knows pain and brokenness, but finds in his or her Africanness the power of justice, mercy, and love, which is inherited from the past—in the blood of one's ancestors—a power that gains strength from others and life from *Mwari*, one's God.

Another central dimension of this African Christian approach to cross-cultural ministry is to see that the poor are given the Bible, and that in it they can discover for themselves God's action in history and in their experience. The aim is to bring awareness and commitment to the fact that, like those in the Bible stories, they too can become agents of God. The intent here is to press home the point that it is within their reach through the power of God to reorder society, to bring about justice and equality, and to foster a

108

spirit of openness and sharing that transcends racial, tribal, gender, and nepotistic boundaries.

An African Understanding of Humanness

Augsburger makes a fundamental distinction between the universal, the cultural, and the unique, quoting Kluckhohn and Murray's statement that "every person is in certain respects (a) like all others, (b) like some others, and (c) like no other."[7] These three dimensions of being human form the basis of a genuine and authentic cross-cultural ministry, and to ignore any one of them is to jeopardize the effectiveness of such a ministry.

The first dimension presupposes the commonality of all humanness. This acknowledgment has implications that go very far. Once adopted in the scheme of a ministry, it opens a new world. It is a starting point of a person's incarnation into the world of another. This assumption carries no sign of arrogance, because one knows that other peoples' values and religions are legitimate.

We Africans show this sense of universality. We believe in a center called *Guruuswa*, a place where all humans come into being. In fact the whole cosmos or universe has *Guruuswa* as its center. From such an understanding we think every human being on earth is ontologically linked to every other, to nature, to spirits, and to God. This notion is based on the principle of the human person-in-relation. This becomes a beginning point for preaching the kingdom of God, which is inclusive and does not denigrate others.

The second dimension concerns what can be called culture. Every human being is shaped, formed, patterned by his or her community. As Augsburger puts it, "This matrix of values, beliefs, customs, religion and basic life assumptions which we call culture is shared with and similar to those who share that community."[8] This presupposes that the person

109

from another culture is different in that he or she holds a different perspective. In order to exercise a fruitful cross-cultural ministry one must be able to appreciate the other's perspective.

Augsburger terms this deliberate affective response "empathy" or "interpathy."[9] By empathy he means a sharing of the other person's feelings through compassionate active imagination. It is not the same as the spontaneous automatic reaction of sympathy, but a choice to transpose oneself into another's world in self-conscious awareness of the other person's consciousness. The advantage of this approach in cross-cultural ministry is its ability to respect the distinctness of self vis-à-vis the other person. This is the same ability we notice in the African principle of existence-in-relation, where one's existence is understood, but in relation to the other person or group. The underlying purpose of the African principle is to enhance rather than diminish cultural boundaries. In this sense the African principle can be used side by side with Augsburger's notion of empathy. Thus, both approaches are crucial in cross-cultural ministry, because in both, the "otherness" of people is recognized. "Otherness" is important because it enables effective human relations to be realized and guaranteed.

Interpathy is somewhat different from empathy, in the sense that it embraces empathy—"feeling with"—together with "thinking with" another person or group. Here one enters, as it were, the other person's world of assumptions, beliefs, and values, and temporarily takes them as one's own. This understanding also resonates with the African notion of existence-in-relation. Both carry the possibility of a pastor's self-incarnation into the life of a local church without diminishing self, culture, or past. Hence, a pastor employing the principle of existence-in-relation using interpathy extends empathy beyond known boundaries of grace. As we see in Augsburger, this grace draws no lines, refuses limits, and claims universal humanness. Such grace in any ministry manifests its ultimate source—the loving God incarnate in the human situation through Jesus Christ by the power of the Holy Spirit.

The third dimension, which asserts that every person is like no other, assumes that each of us is a unique world of perceptions, feelings, and experience. The main focus here is the individual person, with a personal history distinct from every other person's gifts, strengths, and weaknesses, and a self-conscious center of life-experience never replicated by another.[10] Although the African emphasizes belonging to a community or existence in relation to others, the emphasis is not necessarily in conflict with this dimension. For, by the logic of existence-in-relation, the African not only maintains a vital relation with God, ancestors, clan, and family, but also exists in solidarity with each individual member of his or her group. This means that in undertaking cross-cultural ministry in Africa one has no alternative but to recognize and respect individuals and the experiences, gifts, and history unique to them.

Thus it can be seen that in carrying out ministry in Africa—or in any local congregation for that matter—it is of paramount importance to take all three of these dimensions into account.

We are here using the term *cross-cultural* to mean a process whereby we deliberately cross over to another person's perspective or into another community's culture or world view. This implies that every ministry in a given parish or community is cross-cultural. This also means that one will be undertaking cross-cultural ministry even if one is a pastor among a people whose culture is his or her own. The assumption is that, just like persons, each parish is unique, having its own life patterns, customs, rules, and forms of liturgy. Hence, the parish is a culture of its own and must be entered into and related to from the perspective of cross-cultural ministry as outlined in this essay.

111

Cross-Cultural Ministry in Zimbabwe

My ministry will be carried out in Zimbabwe among the Shona and Ndebele tribes, the only two tribes in the whole country. Besides the apparent fact that we are products of African culture, we are also, because of our history of long colonization, children of what has been referred to already as "colonial culture." This is a culture whose institutions are in every way designed to inculcate in the oppressed the feeling and acceptance of both the "superiority" of the white man and the "inferiority" of the African.

On the religious plane, ministry is carried out in a situation where the church has distorted the Shona and Ndebele world views with profound effects on the people. The church has condemned all that is African. The African traditional religion is conceived as nothing but pagan and demonic. By thus looking down on traditional African beliefs, the message of "Christianity" has conspired with the state to create in the African a sense of self-rejection and dejection. At the same time, it has created the white Zimbabwean with a deep sense of conceit and an image of self-superiority.

The Africans have been regarded as primitive and uncivilized with no tinge of enlightenment. The implications of this go very far. An African personality is fostered that accepts these distortions as truth and reality. None of us has escaped this injury, and we bear the wounds in various ways. The colonial culture does not allow the African to be independent. This feeling of being subject does not disappear with the coming of political independence. This acceptance of "inferiority" which inhibits Africans from living their lives freely and fully takes a long time to disappear.

The Zimbabwean context of colonial culture is one in which whiteness is celebrated and blackness is perceived as less-than-human, even by the Africans themselves. Africans are led to believe that whiteness is the norm of being human, and that not to be white is a cultural deviation. Through deliberate effort in cross-cultural ministry, we can help one another to reverse and ultimately eradicate the typical traits of oppressed people, who through long subjugation have assimilated these dehumanizing images of the oppressor.

This is also a situation where after independence the poor continue to be victims of unequal political, economic, and social power. Independence in Zimbabwe for a majority of the people is stressful rather than liberating. Only a few enjoy the essential goods of society. Authority and power remain inaccessible to the people who are poor. It is in this kind of unjust and unequal situation that the cross-cultural ministry based on the African principles of existence-in-relation and *Guruuswa* must be carried out.

A Theology of the Stomach

In the African world we have images that illustrate who Christ is and the role of the community that embodies existence-in-relation. African social solidarity with those in pain or suffering is best expressed in the value the African gives to the place of the stomach in the physico-ethical system.[11] Here the stomach, or the internal organs as a whole, are closely identified with the suffering of the other.

This image is usually associated with the belief that the African who lacks "stomach" has all kinds of evil lurking in and around him or her. On the other hand, to have "stomach" is to exist in clear moral awareness, to be merciful, taking the initiative to do good, to help the person in need, to empathize with the other person, and to be able to suffer with or for other people. This image presupposes that we are cosufferers, and that we perceive all suffering to be relational or social.

What does this mean theologically? This understanding leads us to say that the African God, who exists in relation with people and the whole community, as well as with

113

individuals, is fully incarnate in the painful realities of all of creation. *Mwari*-God is conceived to be a God with power sufficient to overcome evil and suffering.

How does this compare with the Christian notion of God? What is important here is that the African God and the activity of the community are similar to the image of Christ, the crucified and the risen. Through the cross we see not only that God is love, but also that God endures our pain and suffers wounds—God's own scars. So the cross presupposes a God who comes into our situation and experience with wounds and grace.

To think of God in this manner is to presuppose the God who relates to us, who is for us, and who feels for us. In the Resurrection, Jesus shows his scars to Thomas. Those scars belong to his pre-Resurrection existence. Yet according to Marjorie Suchocki, they are the result of the pain and death still present in the Resurrection.[12] Here we have an image of God who comes to us as a wounded healer and at the same time exists in relation to creation.

Richard Shaull, in *Heralds of a New Reformation*, presents the image of a God who reverses or reorders society.[13] In the African world view, people are involved in this reversing and reordering action in the sense that within the people themselves there is a healing force which resonates with God's power of healing. This is where the oppressed draw power to participate in their own liberation.[14]

In the Gospels we not only encounter Christ's action in calling for the reversal of unjust social conditions, but we also see that he himself is such a reversal. Therefore, through his own reversal of values and his proclamation of the gospel, he reveals the nature of God and God's reign.[15] We see this reversal in his acceptance of the lame, the blind, the deaf, in his reaching out to the shunned, and in his openness to women.

114

Conclusion:
An African Approach to Cross-Cultural Ministry

An African approach to cross-cultural ministry based on the principle of existence-in-relation will seek to bring about an awareness in people that leads them to a commitment to action to remove them from a "colonial culture" and into a state of freedom. This approach begins with the African paradigm of the human person-in-relation, and will move to share the assumption of the commonalities of all humankind.

The point here is to stress that we are just like anyone else in the world. After all, in Zimbabwe, people fought their own war of independence. We can use that as a basis to emphasize that all persons need continuously to fight for their own rights, and that justice and equitable order do not come without struggling for them.

Like the people of Latin America described by Shaull, persons must be led to discover for themselves the biblical stories of liberation and social transformation.[16] The intent of the pastor as wounded healer is to share with the wounded in such a way that those who have been silent begin to speak with their own voices. Once oppressed persons recognize that the Jesus of their situation is one who seeks the reversal or reordering of unjust social institutions, they will nurture the moral awareness of "stomach" through identification with the suffering of others. This in turn will empower them to carry out their existence-in-relation in acts of compassion (cosuffering) that join with Jesus in the reversal and reordering which seeks to transform this world into the kingdom of God.

Notes

1. This story is similar to one told by Melva Wilson Costen in "African Roots of Afro-American Baptismal Practices," in "The Black Christian Worship Experience: A Consultation," *The Journal of the Interdenominational Theological Center* (Atlanta: ITC Press, 1986), p. 31.

115

2. Swailem Sidhom, "The Theological Estimate of Man," in Kwesi A. Dickson, ed., *Biblical Revelation and African Beliefs* (London: Lutterworth Press, 1969), p. 102.
3. David W. Augsburger, *Pastoral Counseling Across Cultures* (Philadelphia: Westminster Press, 1986), pp. 368-72.
4. Ibid., p. 369.
5. Ibid., p. 73.
6. Donald E. Messer, *Contemporary Images of Christian Ministry* (Nashville: Abingdon Press, 1989), pp. 86-88.
7. Augsburger, *Pastoral Counseling*, p. 49.
8. Ibid.
9. Ibid., p. 27.
10. Ibid., p. 63.
11. Cf. Adeolu E. A. Adegbola, "The Theological Basis of Ethics," in Kwesi A. Dickson, ed., *Biblical Revelation and African Beliefs* (London: Lutterworth Press, 1969), p. 125.
12. Marjorie H. Suchocki, *God Christ Church* (New York: Crossroad Publishing Co., 1989), p. 114.
13. *Heralds of a New Reformation* (Scottdale, Pa.: Herald Press, 1984), p. 123.
14. Ibid.
15. Cf. Suchocki, *God Christ Church*, p. 92.
16. Shaull, *Heralds of a New Reformation*, pp. 122, 126.

CHAPTER EIGHT

The Ministry as Cross-Cultural Communication

—Douglas E. Wingeier

Douglas E. Wingeier is serving as Professor of Practical Theology at G-ETS, having earned an S.T.B. and Ph.D. from Boston University School of Theology. Dr. Wingeier has ten years' pastoral experience in Massachusetts, and seven years of missionary experience associated with Trinity Theological College in Singapore as professor, Dean of Students, and Director of Field Education. He has also done teaching, research, and consultation in Haiti, Israel and the West Bank, Western Samoa, and South Korea. He has led travel seminars to the People's Republic of China and a work team to Nicaragua. He has traveled widely in Asia, the South Pacific, Europe, the Caribbean, and Latin America, and speaks fluent Chinese.

In this essay, which was first published in The Circuit Rider, *Wingeier draws on his extensive cross-cultural experience to devise a theology of ministry based on Paul's* kenosis *doctrine in Philippians 2. Contending that every congregation is a unique culture, Wingeier develops the thesis that "the ministry . . . is communication out of an ancient culture to one of several contemporary ones, through the medium of a third—that of the pastor him/herself."*

The several skills for cross-cultural communication he enumerates fall into the three categories of asking, listening, and witnessing. The article concludes with several implications for an "emptying-for-filling style of ministry," stressing the importance of entering the cultural life-world of the congregation on their own terms, and offering the gifts and insights of one's own culture to the other.

Such an approach to ministry, understood as essentially cross-cultural communication, follows the dictum of Paul urging us to become "all things to all people," so as to "win more of them" (I Cor. 9:22, 19).

In his first year out of seminary, Dan B. is serving a congregation of factory workers, salespeople, and part-time farmers in a small New England mill town. Because he has been in school all his life, his world has been made up of books, lectures, and intellectual stimulation. Now, suddenly, he is thrust into a new world. It is hard to have a study group because members work different shifts at the mill. Few teenagers think of going on to college. People read little beyond the newspaper headlines. Dan has moved from one culture into another.

Rosemary B. is minister of Christian education in a 3000-member city church and also serves as denominational campus minister at the local university. The nucleus of her congregation, older members who built this church stone by stone with their own hands, are intensely loyal, close-knit, and possessive. Younger families who have joined more recently want the building used to serve the community, which is in transition. The students do not really care about the church; they live on campus and are concerned about studies, personal problems, and career choices. Rosemary must try to understand the background, feelings, and needs of each of these cultures.

Albert R. has a two-point charge—a stable church in a resort community and a congregation of Native Americans six miles out of town. He ministers to three cultures—the conservative, dependable year-round population, the city dwellers who escape to the lake each summer, and the Native Americans, who are trying to maintain their heritage and at the same time make it in the white man's world. Albert is involved in cross-cultural communication every day.

Dan, Rosemary, and Albert regularly stand in the pulpit and lead Bible study groups with their people. In this role, they must delve into the culture and thought-forms of the ancient Hebrew and Greco-Roman worlds out of which the words of Scripture have come and then translate those words into meanings relevant today to the cultures in which they minister. A Bible study on hope will be prepared very differently for Dan's mill workers from one prepared for Rosemary's university congregation. And even though Albert may preach the same sermon in both his churches, it is highly probable that his townsfolk, city visitors, and Native Americans will hear three quite different messages.

The ministry of preaching and teaching, then, is communication out of an ancient culture to one of several modern ones, through the medium of a third—that of the pastor himself or herself.

These situations are not fictitious. Those of Dan and Rosemary were just like my own experiences at earlier points in my ministry. I know of Albert's circumstances firsthand. Although I was aware there were communication problems in those situations, it was not until I had experience in an entirely different culture overseas that I recognized *all* ministry is essentially cross-cultural communication. My seven years in Singapore, serving as teacher and pastor there, taught me that effective ministry involves awareness of the implicit assumptions and behavior patterns of one's own culture, growing understanding of the customs and thought-forms of one's adopted culture, and the translation of meanings from the biblical life-world through one's own filters into the experience of another people.

It takes more than common sense and intuition to accomplish this cross-cultural translation. Both a theological foundation and some communication skills are needed.

A Theology of Emptying-for-Filling

The *kenosis* doctrine of Paul in Philippians 2 provides a clue for a theology of cross-cultural communication. Christians are enjoined to "let the same mind be in you that was in Christ Jesus, who, though he was in the form of God, / did not regard equality with God / as something to be exploited, / but emptied himself, / taking the form of a slave, / being born in human likeness" (5-7).

In order to communicate God's reconciling purpose, the Son emptied himself of the forms of his heavenly context and took on the mode and customs of those he was going to. He was less concerned with holding onto his accustomed way of life than with making plain God's new possibilities for human existence. The fullness of communication required an emptying of familiar patterns and a naked entering into a different world. "He humbled himself / and became obedient to the point of death— / even death on a cross" (v. 8), because he knew that only by accepting the limits of a particular culture could he communicate the universal, transcendent, fulfilling life in God's grace. Only by being willing to be defined and judged by one people could he give expression to the Life which defines and judges all people.

This is cross-cultural communication—divesting oneself of the cultural trappings out of which one comes in order to enter fully into the life of another people. Like Paul, we seek to "become all things to all people, that [we] might by all means save some" (I Cor. 9:22).

In one sense, this aspiration sounds both undesirable and impossible. Our identity is too closely tied up with our cultural origins and values to be readily wished away for the sake of identifying with a new people. But Jesus did not forsake his integrity. He told the people to whom he went, "You have heard that it was said to those of ancient times. . . . But I say to you . . ." (Matt. 5:21 ff.). He became

120

a Jew without submerging his identity in their culture. He became one with them in order to communicate to them a Word from beyond their culture. And Paul identified with those both within and outside the law, "for the sake of the gospel" (I Cor. 9:23), that is, in order to communicate the Word and win them to a loyalty higher than either of their present cultures.

The essential strategy is not to deny or disguise one's cultural roots and identity, but to avoid cultural imperialism. The sensitive pastor recognizes the riches in all cultures, is open to listening and learning from them, and rejects any expression of arrogance or presumption, which always blocks the giving and receiving of cultural gifts. Like Paul, we understand that to have credibility in another culture, we must enter into it as fully as possible so that people can say "This person is one of us." But also like Paul, we will "not be conformed to this world, but be transformed by the renewing of [our] minds, so that [we] may discern what is the will of God" (Rom. 12:2).

The *kenosis* of Jesus, the Word made flesh, then, provides a biblical model for ministry as cross-cultural communication. One preserves one's identity and avoids becoming a chameleon by being grounded in the Word and continuing the never-ending task of distinguishing the *kerygma* from the cultural forms in which it has always been expressed.

Skills for Cross-Cultural Communication

The skills needed are asking, listening, and witnessing. The *asking* implies a willingness to let the other persons speak first. We ask how they feel, what they believe, and who they are. We want to know them, to appreciate and accept them for who they are. As a first step, we are willing to empty ourselves of our presuppositions and enter the dialogue on the others' terms.

The asking is accompanied by attentive *listening* to what the

121

other is saying. We let it be known that we are hearing and grasping the other's self-statement. Because we are listening to the pouring out of a life, we focus our attention on the person who is revealing to us who he or she is. By use of such phrases as "I hear you saying," "You seem to be feeling," and "What I'm hearing now is," we let the other know that we are listening and also check whether we are hearing correctly.

While asking about and listening to the other's statement, we are also making our own. We bear *witness* to who we are and where we stand. We do not make our statement in an arrogant way, which implies that it is superior to that of the other, nor do we try to impose it. We offer it in a spirit of humility and openness, asking for response and dialogue. We give an "I-message," telling how things look to us, without presuming that others must see them our way. Although this approach to witnessing does not seek to force conversions, the modest, unassuming attitude it projects does commend us and our statement to others for serious consideration.

Implications for a Style of Ministry

For Dan, Rosemary, and Albert to minister effectively in their respective situations, they need to adopt an emptying-for-filling style of ministry. This will involve:

1. *Entering the cultural life-world or life-worlds of the congregation on their own terms.* We must learn all we can from and about our setting. We must not assume that words and behavior mean to them what they mean to us, but we must check things out. We must let down our guard, throw off our biases, and let the culture we are entering influence us to the full.

2. *Allowing time for reflection.* This influence can be overwhelming. We run the risk of losing our identity by a too ready and uncritical acceptance of another culture. To spend time in reflection permits us to see the similarities,

122

differences, and points of intersection between our beliefs and behavior patterns and theirs. We begin to discover where and how we can make our witness, while continuing to ask sensitively and listen carefully.

3. *Examining our culture from the standpoint of the other.* This helps us discover how the way we think and express ourselves has been conditioned by previous experience. It reminds us of the limitations of our own understanding and helps us become more open to insights coming from the other culture.

4. *Waiting a year to act.* It will take at least one year to get an accurate reading on the culture we have entered. We may discover fairly quickly that people start on time, accept responsibility, but take no initiative, or resist singing unfamiliar hymns. But it will take much longer to find out what this means. It is risky to act on first impressions. We do better to let the church run itself for a year while we watch for, listen for, and learn who is influential, what is important to people, and how things get done. Once we understand the way things are, we then can establish priorities for action and begin to make a telling witness. By first listening, we will have earned the right to be heard.

5. *Adopting their folkways and thought-forms.* As the Word became flesh in order to give expression to God's love, so must we take on the language and life patterns of our people as a means of communicating the gospel. To appreciate another culture from the inside is a stimulus to significant growth. To use frequent "God-talk" or give up smoking or ride the commuter train or empathize with both farmers and migrant farmhands will help to establish a climate in which genuine communication about the meaning of the gospel can take place. And when confrontation is called for, as it surely will be, we can be assured they will hear what we have to say, both because we have listened to them and because we will be speaking their language, and not our own.

6. *Enabling people to make their own meanings.* For persons to relate their faith to their cultural context, they need to learn to think theologically about their lives. But they will not be able to do this if we pastors insist on doing their thinking for them. Rather, we need to ask questions that encourage searching, to identify cultural filters, to accept doctrinal differences and respect those who hold them, and to trust laypersons to make their own meanings with integrity and faithfulness.

7. *Offering the gifts and insights of our culture to the other.* Just as our culture can be judged and enriched by the perspectives of another, so is the reverse also true. Cultures become ingrown and need feedback from others to help them criticize and reformulate their patterns of thinking and doing. Once we have achieved a relationship of credibility and trust with our congregations by entering and affirming their world, we can begin to share some of the ideas and approaches of our own. This will enable them to examine their own cultural presuppositions and to assimilate some of the values and practices we have made appealing to them.

Clearly, Dan, Rosemary, Albert, and others like them can benefit from practicing the emptying-for-filling style of ministry. By practicing the ministry of cross-cultural communication, we become "all things to all people," and in this way "win more of them" (I Cor. 9:22, 19).

PART THREE:
EXPERIENCE

CHAPTER NINE

Learning About Ministry from the Two-thirds World

—Douglas E. Wingeier

In this article, Dr. Wingeier writes about ministry as he has encountered it in several countries in the "Two-thirds World." In a Samoan proverb, "The pathway to authority is through service," he discovers a cultural parallel to Jesus' modeling of the servant style of ministry, which gave him an authority different from that of the scribes.

In Korea, Wingeier sees ministry grounded in frequent, fervent prayer and mobilized through effective organization. The influence of Shamanism in this same country evokes a sense of mystery and excitement, and the Korean folk dances of working people give expression to social protest against injustice and oppression—both significant dimensions of ministry.

The intense suffering and courageous faithfulness of the church in West China, and its dynamic leadership by an aging though still-active pastor, exemplify for Wingeier the ministry of witness through persecution. And the Ecclesial Base Communities in Nicaragua give expression to a spirituality of solidarity and struggle that demonstrates a ministry grounded in biblical reflection, focused on lay empowerment, and identified with the struggles of the people for justice and liberation.

These vignettes of significant dimensions of ministry do not pretend to offer a comprehensive model for the North American church. But, combined with relevant Scripture as they are, they do point the way toward central ministry emphases, which can well be emulated as the church in this country increasingly discovers itself to be in a missionary situation and revises its approach to ministry accordingly.

In recent years it has been my good fortune to sojourn in a number of countries around the world, living and working with Christians there in ways making it possible for me to come to understand and appreciate their approaches to ministry. The traditional missionary posture in these interactions has been for the Westerner to be the teacher and persons in so-called mission lands to be the learners. But, while I usually went in the role of a teacher or consultant, the roles were often reversed and I ended up learning much more than I was able to contribute.

The lands and churches I visited were in Latin America, Asia, and the South Pacific. They have been variously called developing nations, receiving churches, younger churches, and Third World countries. But all of these terms are less than respectful of the gifts they offer and of the important position they occupy in the world. The term "Two-thirds World" more accurately describes their numerical predominance and also suggests their cultural significance.

The ministry themes learned from the Two-thirds World discussed in this article are: authority through service as seen in Western Samoa; the discipline of prayer and organization, encountered in Korea; participation in mystery and protest, also learned in Korea; witness through persecution, discovered in China; and a spirituality of solidarity and struggle, experienced in Nicaragua.

Authority Through Service: Western Samoa

While teaching for five months at Piula Theological College in Western Samoa, I became acquainted with a well-known Samoan proverb: "The pathway to authority is through service." Since the Samoan word for authority can be translated as leadership and power as well as authority, the proverb is really saying that "the way to authority, leadership, and power is through service."

The Samoan culture is quite hierarchical and patriarchal. Each extended family or clan is headed by a *matai* or chief, who rules and is served by the *aomaga* or untitled men, as well as by the women and children. The untitled men must perform faithful service in their younger years if they aspire ever to become a chief. One who has learned well to conform to expectations and carry out duties and responsibilities is viewed as a reliable candidate to become a leader and exercise power over and on behalf of the extended family. Hence, one must serve dutifully in order to gain a position of authority.

Jesus must have been addressing a similar cultural pattern in the following incident:

> A dispute also arose among them as to which one of them was to be regarded as the greatest. But he said to them, "The kings of the Gentiles lord it over them; and those in authority over them are called benefactors. But not so with you; rather the greatest among you must become like the youngest, and the leader like one who serves. For who is greater, the one who is at the table or the one who serves? Is it not the one at the table? But I am among you as one who serves." (Luke 22:24-27)

The reference to sitting at table and serving has a direct parallel in Samoan society. Because the Samoan people converted to Christianity en masse with their chiefs more than 150 years ago, the village chiefs are also elders in the church today. After church on Sunday they gather in the pastor's home for a feast called a *toonai*, which has been prepared before dawn by the *aomaga*. It is served by them as well, as the *matai* sit in a circle on straw mats in the *fale*, the Samoan thatched roof house open on all sides. A flick of the hand or a sucking noise made with the mouth will bring a server to the chief's place in an instant to respond to whatever request is made. Other untitled men sit before the chiefs waving away the flies

129

with banana leaf fans as the meal progresses. When the chiefs
are through, the food is taken away by the *aomaga*, who then
eat the ample leftovers in a nearby *fale*, followed by the women
and children. Clearly, the chiefs who sit at table are ranked as
greater than those who serve.

Though not so markedly hierarchical, our society also ranks
persons according to position, income, and social status.
Worth, esteem, and often power and authority are accorded
to persons in proportion to salary level, rank in the
institution, or the suburb or street where one lives.

Jesus calls his followers to be counter-cultural—to challenge the norms and conventions of society by choosing the
servant role. When the disciples were arguing over who
would sit at his right and left in the heavenly kingdom, he
rebuked them, saying:

> You know that the rulers of the Gentiles lord it over them, and
> their great ones are tyrants over them. It will not be so among
> you; but whoever wishes to be great among you must be your
> servant, and whoever wishes to be first among you must be
> your slave; just as the Son of Man came not to be served but to
> serve, and to give his life a ransom for many. (Matt. 20:25-28)

Both by word and by example, Jesus calls us to adopt the
servant role. At the Last Supper Jesus took the towel and
basin and washed the disciples' feet, explaining to them:

> So if I, your Lord and Teacher, have washed your feet, you
> also ought to wash one another's feet. For I have set you an
> example that you also should do as I have done to you. Very
> truly, I tell you, servants are not greater than their master.
> (John 13:14-16*a*)

Jesus' modeling of the servant style of ministry is caught up
in this hymn of the early church, which exhorts us to:

> Let the same mind be in you that was in Christ Jesus,
>   who, though he was in the form of God,

did not regard equality with God
as something to be exploited,
but emptied himself,
taking the form of a slave,
being born in human likeness.
And being found in human form,
he humbled himself
and became obedient to the point of death—
even death on a cross. (Phil. 2:5-8)

Servanthood is central to the New Testament understanding of ministry. It is not seen, however, as a weak or bemeaning role, or a position one is forced to assume against one's will. Rather, one chooses to make oneself available to meet the needs of others.

Through adopting a loving, caring stance and sacrificially offering oneself to meet human need, one gains an authority greater than that accorded by social rank or status. It was said of Jesus that "he taught them as one having authority, and not as the scribes" (Mark 1:22). The authority of inner integrity and authenticity is greater than the outer authority of position. Those who devote their time and energy to responding to the needs of other human beings are willingly respected, appreciated, listened to, and followed, while those who use their power and authority to command respect and obedience are only tolerated and feared.

The Samoan proverb is correct. "The pathway to authority *is* through service." But not in the sense of a dutiful conformity to cultural patterns and expectation, in order to earn a titled position and rank later on. Rather, the authority of integrity is gained through a willing choice to make oneself available to meet the needs of others.

There is power and authority in the ministry of service. True leadership, after the pattern of Jesus, is servant leadership.

The Discipline of Prayer and Organization: Korea

While I was visiting a Korean church, the pastor took me into his study and showed me a photo album containing pictures of all the family units in his congregation. He told me that he takes this album into his daily prayer time and prays for a number of these families by name each day, with their pictures before him. His congregation knows of this practice, with the result that they respond positively and enthusiastically to his pastoral leadership, knowing that their pastor is a person of prayer and that he is praying for them.

Korean pastors and a solid core of laity arise before dawn each day to attend five o'clock prayer meetings in their churches. Weekly evening prayer meetings are also held, and the network of class meetings devotes a significant portion of its weekly gatherings to prayer. The ministry and mission of the church, and the witness of individual members, are undergirded by frequent and widespread prayer support.

Every member of every congregation belongs to a class meeting. Each group has a lay leader, who attends weekly training sessions devoted to leadership cultivation and training, prayer for the needs of and reports on individual members, and specific preparation for leading that week's meeting.

The class leaders are trained by and accountable to the pastor, or, in larger churches, to women evangelists called "Bible women," who in turn report to associate pastors, and they to the senior pastor. An hour after the last Sunday worship service the senior pastor has a report on his desk of all the absentees in all the class groups. Individual concerns become the subject of prayer, both in their own groups and throughout the congregation. Pastoral follow-up calls are made early the next week, by either class leader, Bible woman, or one of the pastors.

Evangelism also takes place through this network of

132

neighborhood groups meeting in homes. Members invite their friends and neighbors to attend the weekly meetings, and newcomers are led step by step into the fuller life of the congregation and into a commitment to Christ from this point of entry. The class meeting thus becomes a built-in support group to help them with their struggles and adjustments, possibly in connection with a move from country to city or from Korea to the United States.

The discipline of both prayer and accountability is very high in the class meeting and in the Korean congregation. Regular attendance at class meeting, prayer meeting, and worship service is expected of all members, as are tithing and Bible study.

When first entering the group, persons may know very little about the Christian faith. But through attendance at several meetings and services each week they are exposed to much Christian guidance, instruction, and community life, so conversions regularly take place and they are socialized into the faith community fairly rapidly. The expectations of church membership are high, and the structures of accountability and support strong.

The result is a Korean church that is growing very rapidly—both in that country and this. Tithing by nearly all members makes funds available to these growing congregations to engage in evangelistic and missional outreach. The discipline of prayer and organization supports people in the new spiritual covenants they make and holds them accountable to them.

This pattern is based on the class meeting structure devised by John Wesley, but it also bears a remarkable similarity to the early church as described in Acts 1 and 2. Between the Resurrection and Pentecost, the disciples met regularly in an upper room and devoted themselves to prayer and Bible study. This close-knit community provided support and accountability as they sought God's guidance on how to carry out the mission Jesus had given

133

them. Both guidance and power came on Pentecost, and the rest is history.

If we have not learned it from the New Testament, perhaps we can learn from the Korean church. Small groups of Christians who regularly gather for prayer, Bible study, reflection on Christ's call to discipleship, and support and accountability for faithful witness and missional outreach, are the lifeblood of the church.

Participation in Mystery and Protest: Korea

Because the culture and tradition of Shamanism are strong in Korea, the church naturally partakes of many of its characteristics. To understand the uniqueness of Korean Christianity one must try to enter into the Shamanistic ethos. To do this I attended a *kut*, the rite of petition, offering, and blessing characteristic of Korean Shamanism.

The all-day ceremony was led by three Shamans, one man, two women, all dressed in colorful flowing robes. The ceremony proceeded through a series of cycles of communication between the petitioner and the spirits through the medium of the Shamans. Each cycle began with a petition to the spirits for relief from the problems faced and a blessing for future well-being. This was followed by a scolding of the petitioner for past unfaithfulness, an offering of money, food, and drink to placate the spirits, a rite of expulsion of the evil spirits, and finally a blessing and promise of future good fortune.

As the day moved along, the sense of excitement and community grew, friends and observers (myself included) were invited to participate in the meal and dancing, the prayers and incantations grew louder and more exuberant, and the support and good feeling for the petitioner became more pronounced.

Several features characterize this Korean folk religion: (1) A sense of excitement, mystery, and ecstasy—called *shinnanda* or *hng*—pervades the group, and particularly the Shaman,

134

who is caught up in the spirit and becomes its mouthpiece. (2) The *kut* takes place on the village ground or in a home—the place of the common people—not in a temple or holy place. There is no separation between the sacred and the secular; the spiritual and material worlds are one. (3) The relationship between human beings and the spirits is one of harmony and balance, which is disrupted by human disobedience or neglect, and restored through offerings of food, drink, money, compliments, and praise. Further, (4) the community participates fully in the rite—in eating, drinking, dancing, and fellowship. A spirit of community, belonging, good feeling, and celebration pervades the event. And (5) the gods and spirits are not hierarchical. Spirits of animals, trees, places, and ancestors all are called upon in no apparent order or rank. They are approachable, accommodating, and anthropomorphic in their susceptibility to flattery and placation.

The Shaman—or *mudang,* as the women Shamans, who make up about two-thirds of all Korean Shamans, are called—is the intermediary between the earthly and spirit realms, passing freely and frequently between the two during the course of the *kut.* She or he is the "mystagogue" or "symbol-bearer" (cf. Urban T. Holmes, *The Priest in Community*) who accompanies other human beings into the "boundary experiences" of life when they face the "abyss" of nonbeing, pain, and loss in various kinds of misfortune.

The Shaman is a low-status and despised role in Korean society, and parents strongly discourage their daughters from entering the profession. However, many who become Shamans have undergone a spiritual calling through a profound experience of physical illness, emotional disturbance, or vision, and are impelled to take up the practice almost against their will.

Shamans serve four functions: (1) They act as priests, mediating between human beings and gods and spirits; (2) they offer healing and exorcism, expelling bad spirits to bring relief from physical and mental pain, grief, and distress;

(3) they explain abnormal phenomena and predict both bad and good fortune; and (4) they arrange for recreation, providing communal good times of singing, dancing, eating, and drinking, as persons (mostly from the lower classes) participate together in festive occasions.

Shamanism provides the oppressed and hard-working farmers and laborers of traditional Korean society with occasions for community, celebration, restoration of harmony and balance, forgiveness and reconciliation, and relief from oppressive circumstances. It promises the blessing of the gods and spirits in the form of material prosperity or at least relief from suffering, in return for material offerings and faithful observance of religious rites and practices to satisfy the divine demands and expectations.

Shamanism is closely linked in traditional Korean culture with other forms of celebration, escape from drudgery, and protest against injustice and oppression, such as that of the farmer's dance and the masked dance. The farmer's dance, performed at festival times with boundless energy, exquisite precision, colorful costumes, banners, streamers, and the loud music of drums and cymbals, gives expression to the native creativity, joy, and dignity of working people. In today's Korean society, farmers, workers, and students are recovering this indigenous art form and adapting it to present-day circumstances. I witnessed one dance, for example, that depicted workers and capitalists in a life-and-death struggle, with the workers emerging victorious amidst great joy and celebration.

The masked dance depicts representatives of the peasant class as repeatedly outsmarting the wealthy and educated elite *(yangbans)* and the Buddhist priests, who come across as idiotic buffoons. Jokes, songs, and commentary, spoken by the performers behind their masks in the course of the dance, give expression to the workers' resentment of their oppressors. This art form was apparently tolerated by the ruling class as a relatively harmless form of social protest, but it did—and does—serve to maintain the morale and solidarity of the workers and peasants in the midst of their life of exploitation and hardship.

These expressions of mystery, ecstasy, mutuality, support, encouragement, solidarity, and prophetic protest, recall the words quoted by Peter from the prophet Joel on the Day of Pentecost:

> In the last days it will be, God declares,
> that I will pour out my Spirit upon all flesh,
>   and your sons and your daughters shall prophesy,
> and your young men shall see visions,
>   and your old men shall dream dreams.
> Even upon my slaves, both men and women,
>   in those days I will pour out my Spirit;
>   and they shall prophesy.   (Acts 2:17-18)

The Spirit of God inspires the poor and oppressed of society to seek reconciliation and the restoration of harmony, to gain comfort and guidance in the midst of life's boundary experiences, to find the solidarity and encouragement of supportive community, to celebrate life with joy and comedy, to protest injustice and oppression, and to see visions and dream dreams of the kind of world God intends for all of God's children. And ministry involves providing leadership within the faith community to help all this to happen.

Witness Through Persecution: China

Daniel Li Lian Ke is an eighty-eight-year-old pastor in Chengdu, West China, who carries a cane and walks with a decided limp. He went there in 1940 as a refugee, remained during the war with Japan, and then was imprisoned for twenty-some years during and after the Cultural Revolution, when, as he told me, all the churches were closed, occupied, and some torn down, and Christians were persecuted along with intellectuals and any others with ties to the West.

In prison, he reports, they were confined ten to a cell, and slept on the floor. "But," he says, "I was protected; it was those on the outside who received really cruel treatment." He admits, however, that "the reason I cannot walk well today is because all those years in prison I was cold, and had to sleep on the floor in an unheated cell."

Today, released from prison at long last, Daniel Li is the leader of the Christians of Chengdu—chief pastor of the church, principal of the seminary, a saintly, kindly, gentle man who has earned the respect of Christian and non-Christian alike because of his courage in witnessing for his faith in the midst of suffering.

He told me how, when the new government came in in 1980 and instituted freedom of belief and began opening churches again, the leaders of the seven or eight denominations in Chengdu got together and discussed how to begin working together. They decided to unite, in what they call a "post-denominational church"—on the basis of "one Lord, one faith, one baptism" (Eph. 4:5)—and to work together cooperatively without making formal theological or organizational agreements.

We worshiped in a service in which 700 were in attendance and more than 100 new Christians were baptized—only one of several services that Sunday. Then he took us to another church, which had just been rebuilt and would be opened in two weeks, giving the Christians of Chengdu their choice of two places of worship. That new building also housed a seminary, and we met some of the faculty and students. The library consisted of three small bookcases—less than one-fourth the size of my personal library. But under the Reverend Daniel Li's guidance they are setting out to provide training for young Christian leaders of the rapidly growing church in West China for today and tomorrow—

to replace the four pastors of the Chengdu church, all of whom are over eighty.

In Guilin, a city in South China, conversation with the woman pastor and a leading layman revealed that they had devised a unique and innovative mode of evangelism. Forbidden by the government from preaching the gospel outside the church, the laity of that congregation had decided to take turns sitting in the open doorway of the church, which fronted on a busy street. Engaging passersby in conversation, they would share the gospel with them from within the church building, then invite them in to attend classes and services. Twenty had been baptized just the Sunday before we were there.

When I asked Daniel Li of Chengdu how he accounted for the amazing growth of the church in China in recent years—from 700,000 in 1949 when the missionaries left to more than 7,000,000 today, by conservative estimates—he had two answers: the work of the Holy Spirit; and the spiritual hunger of people who, after forty years under Communism, realize that there is more to life than what they can see and touch. Material things are not enough to satisfy; they must seek to live for something higher. The Christian gospel is the only thing in China today pointing to that something higher.

But I suspect that there is a third reason for this growth—the life and witness through suffering, of saints of God like Daniel Li Lian Ke. As stories of the Cultural Revolution era come to light, it is becoming apparent that many Christians—pastors and laity alike—were faithful to God and to the well-being of their own people during those years. In some places, for example, forbidden by the authorities to hold even small group meetings in their homes, they gathered on the streets in twos and threes and prayed with their eyes open, as though they were engaged in casual conversation—so as to maintain their faith and morale without arousing suspicion.

Through these and other acts of quiet courage, faithful

139

witness, and willing sacrifice—inspired by the strength of God in their hearts—they were able to endure suffering, give hope to those about them, "serve the people" (the omnipresent slogan of Maoist China during those years), and earn the undying gratitude and respect of their fellow citizens.

These words of tribute from the epistle to the Hebrews aptly describe Chinese Christians like Daniel Li:

> All of these [lived and] died in faith without having received the promises, but from a distance they saw and greeted them. They confessed that they were strangers and foreigners on the earth, for people who speak [and act] in this way make it clear that they are seeking a homeland. . . . They desire a better country, that is, a heavenly one. Therefore God is not ashamed to be called their God; indeed, [God] has prepared a city for them. (11:13-14, 16)

Ministry for Chinese Christians over the past forty years has involved faithful witness through persecution—remaining obedient to Christ and responsive to the needs of others, enduring imprisonment and suffering with patience and hope, finding creative ways of supporting one another and sharing Christ with their neighbors, and offering a vision of hope and a promise of a reality beyond this world. Through suffering they have sowed the seeds of church renewal, and today many are turning to Christ because they have seen in his followers a joy, strength, and hope that they believe can fill the gap in their own lives.

A Spirituality of Solidarity and Struggle: Nicaragua

The Base Christian Communities of Nicaragua (now called Ecclesial Base Communities to better express their close identification with the church) form a network of revolutionary groups that have effectively united Christian faith with struggle to create a more just society for more than twenty years. They provided leadership to the insurrection that overthrew the dictator Somoza in 1979, have called forth and nurtured the artistic and organizational gifts of the poor, and have contributed many leaders to the Sandinista government. Also called the Church of the Poor, they form the nucleus of leadership of congregations in many urban barrios and rural villages.

Meeting weekly in private homes or church halls, these communities share their experiences of the past week, engage in Bible study related to the realities of their daily struggle and social situation, make plans and assign responsibilities for the religious and community self-help projects they are involved with, and close with a time of prayer for one another and the continuing work of remaking their society into one that serves the needs of *all* the people.

Then, on Sunday, as they gather for worship, the liturgy used is a popular folk mass, with portions prepared by the central office of their movement. The parish priest, instead of preaching a homily, engages them in dialogue around the scripture they discussed during the week, calling forth their insights and applications to their daily lives and social reality.

In one church I visited, the La Merced Roman Catholic parish near the Oriental Market in Managua, Father Antonio Castro, a quiet, soft-spoken Nicaraguan priest, conducted an Easter vigil, which included guitar music from the popular "Misa Campesina," fireworks in the courtyard to celebrate the Resurrection, an open mike for parishioners to share their reflections on the text, communion to the singing of "When the Saints Go Marching In," and the cup held by a small boy for us to dip our wafers in. The people clapped for joy at several points in the service, and the passing of the peace was a time of hugging that lasted several minutes and gave expression to the obviously deep affection that people felt for one another in that community.

The altar and pulpit in the sanctuary were built of the famous Somoza paving bricks *(adoquin)*, like those dug from

141

the streets to form barricades against Somoza's tanks in the successful Sandinista-led 1979 revolution—showing the solidarity of this parish with the struggles and aspirations of the continuing people's revolution.

In talking with Father Castro before the service in his rectory adjoining the church, we saw the young people relating to him as a caring friend and mentor. We also noted the service center attached to his church, which provided community outreach programs such as vocational training for youth, daycare for children, and sewing classes for women. During this visit, we were deeply impressed with his depth of commitment to serving the poor, his fostering of lay participation and leadership, and the creativity and celebrativeness of the worship.

Central to the Base Communities is Bible study, which assumes that the Holy Spirit will lead them to understand the Word and discover new insights. Ernesto Cardenal's *The Gospel in Solentiname* (four volumes) records many of these scripture dialogues from his years leading the communities on the Solentiname islands in Lake Nicaragua. The communities connect the Bible story with their story and struggle in powerful and perceptive ways. Base Community members are empowered through recognizing that they are subjects, persons of worth and dignity, able to think and act for themselves. They become an extended family of faith, and build a new quality of life in community and a sense of family solidarity as they sit in a circle rather than the traditional rows. The leader, whether a priest or a lay Delegate of the Word, serves as a facilitator, not an authoritative interpreter.

The priesthood of all believers, the vocation of all Christians, is lived out in these communities, as they share leadership for their meetings and projects. Among the projects we visited were a soya collective, where women were developing a whole new protein-rich diet with a variety of tasty recipes using soybean flour, a sewing cooperative, a

142

youth activity program, a daycare center, a health clinic using natural medicines and herbs, a lunchroom, and a housing development providing homes for the Mothers of Heroes and Martyrs, among which were those who had lost husbands, sons, homes, and possessions to Contra attacks in the mountains. These Christians freely share their possessions in common as the need arises. Poor though they are, they do not hesitate to invite those less fortunate into their homes and give to them of what little they have.

In the rural areas, where ordained priests are in short supply, the Base Communities are led by Delegates of the Word, lay pastoral agents, both men and women, who are natural leaders in their villages and who use their gifts to serve the community, not dominate others.

The experience of the Nicaraguan Base Communities is also very reminiscent of that of the first-century Christians, as described in Acts 2:42-46:

> They devoted themselves to the apostles' teaching and fellowship, to the breaking of bread and the prayers. Awe came upon everyone, because many wonders and signs were being done by the apostles. All who believed were together and had all things in common; they would sell their possessions and goods and distribute the proceeds to all, as any had need. Day by day, as they spent much time together in the temple, they broke bread at home and ate their food with glad and generous hearts.

And also like the early Christians, the Nicaraguan Christians in the Ecclesial Base Communities gather together not only, or even primarily, for mutual support and uplifting. Rather, their meeting together is for purposes of being equipped to engage in the mission of Jesus, to make humane and transform their society, in obedience to the mandate of Jesus:

143

> The Spirit of the Lord is upon me,
>   because he has anointed me
>   to bring good news to the poor.
> He has sent me to proclaim release to the captives
>   and recovery of sight to the blind,
>   to let the oppressed go free,
> to proclaim the year of the Lord's favor. (Luke 4:18-19)

I was profoundly affected by the deep Christian passion and commitment, keen scriptural insight, courage to struggle, suffer, and die for their faith, and intense Resurrection joy of these Christian sisters and brothers in the Ecclesial Base Communities of Nicaragua. Their undying hope in the face of the continuing violent North American intervention in their homeland made a deep and lasting impression on me. Their forgiving love and dedicated faith called me to make a deeper commitment to joining in their struggle for peace, justice, and liberation. I will never be the same for having lived in their homes and shared in their lives and worship.

Conclusion

Ministry is *service* that exemplifies inner *authority* and thereby earns respect. Ministry is *discipline* grounded in *prayer* and made effective through *organization*. Ministry is participation in rites of *mystery* and acts of *protest*, in which God's power and love are encountered and God's justice is proclaimed. Ministry is *witness* to the power of Christ to overcome suffering and to offer meaning and hope beyond the material world. And ministry is engagement in the continuing *struggle* of the poor, God's people, to *transform* the structures of society into the Realm of God in which the poor hear Good News, the captives are released, the blind recover sight, the oppressed are set free, and God's timetable is announced.

This is what I have learned thus far about ministry from Christian sisters and brothers in the Two-thirds World. I am sure there will be more.